Jerusalem's Holy Ground

"The air over Jerusalem is saturated with prayers and dreams," wrote poet Yehuda Amichai—and they gather like a storm over the plateau called Mount Moriah. To Jews this is the Temple Mount, their holiest site, where the Western Wall survives from the Second Temple era. To Christians it is ground that Jesus walked. To Muslims it is the Haram al-Sharif, the Noble Sanctuary, where the golden Dome of the Rock shelters a scarred outcrop of limestone. The meaning of that rock—linked to Muhammad and his mystical journey to heaven, to Solomon and the First Temple, to David and the Ark of the Covenant, to Abraham and the near sacrifice of his son—is at the heart of what makes this such sacred, and deeply contested, ground.

ca 960 B.C. | SOLOMON'S TEMPLE

At the direction of God, the Bible recounts, Israelite King David built an altar on or near the rock about 1000 B.C. His ambition to erect a Temple to the Lord was fulfilled by his son, King Solomon. Dedicated about 960 B.C., it was destroyed in 586 B.C., when King Nebuchadrezzar sacked Jerusalem and exiled the Jews to Babylon. The Ark of the Covenant, previously enshrined in the Temple's Holy of Holies, vanished from the historical record.

Heralded by a shofar, priests move the Ark of the Covenant into Solomon's Temple on the day of its dedication. The ark held the Commandment tablets that had been given to Moses.

ca 10 B.C. | HEROD'S TEMPLE

Herod the Great, appointed by Rome as King of Judaea, doubled the size of the Temple Mount. The grand limestone temple he dedicated about 10 B.C. was a renovation of the Second Temple, built 500 years earlier when the Jews returned from Babylonian exile. Jesus taught on the Temple Mount in the week before his death, about A.D. 30. In A.D. 70, 6,000 Jews died on the Temple Mount as the Roman army crushed a revolt, torching the Temple and demolishing the complex.

In Jewish tradition, the Mount Moriah rock is revered as the Rock of Sacrifice, on which Abraham, to prove his faith, prepared to offer his son Isaac nearly 4,000 years ago. To Muslims, his son Ishmael was the intended sacrifice.

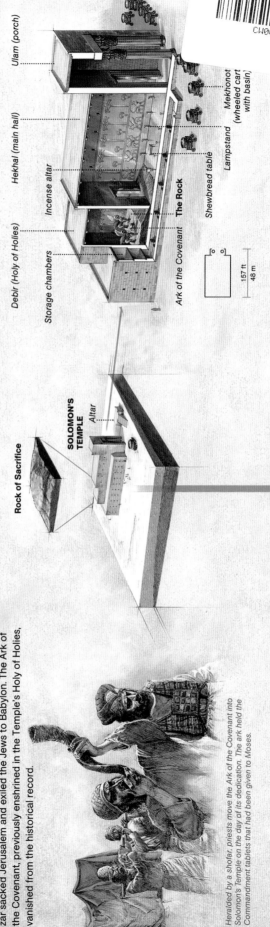

No firm archaeological evidence remains from Solomon's Temple. Scholars base reconstructions on biblical accounts (I Kings and II Chronicles) and on evidence from excavations of other buildings from that era.

Ulam (porch)

Mekhonot
(wheeled cart
with basin)

Lampstand

Hekhal (main hall)

Incense altar

Shewbread table

Debir (Holy of Holies)

The Rock

Storage chambers

Ark of the Covenant

157 ft
48 m

Rock of Sacrifice

SOLOMON'S TEMPLE

Altar

Antonia Fortress

Scholars reconstruct the Temple Mo
archaeological remains, from the w
Jewish historian Flavius Josephus, ;
a code of rabbinic law that holds th
depiction incorporates interpretati

• Structures discovered by
  19th-century explorers

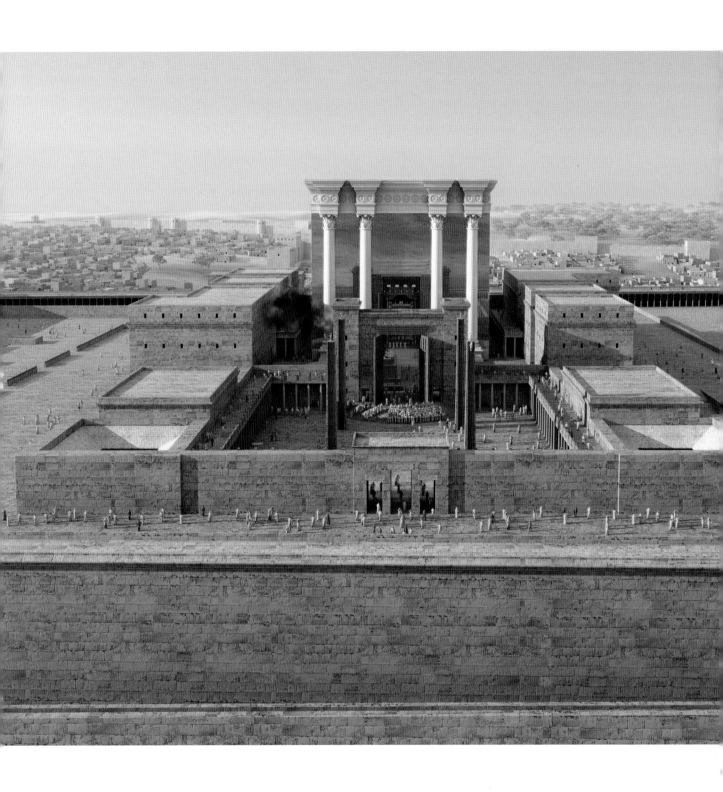

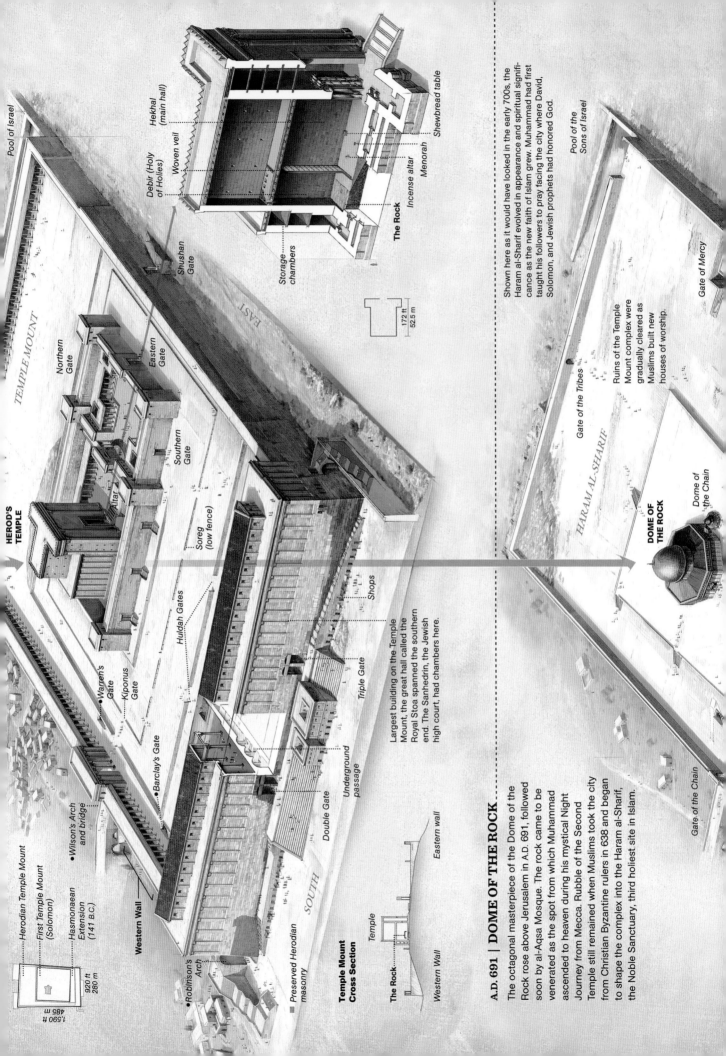

Pool of Israel

TEMPLE MOUNT

HEROD'S TEMPLE

Debir (Holy of Holies)

Hekhal (main hall)

Woven veil

Shushan Gate

Storage chambers

Incense altar

Menorah

Shewbread table

The Rock

172 ft
52.5 m

Northern Gate

Eastern Gate

Southern Gate

Altar

Soreg (low fence)

EAST

Warren's Gate

Kiponus Gate

Barclay's Gate

Huldah Gates

Shops

Triple Gate

Double Gate

Underground passage

Largest building on the Temple Mount, the great hall called the Royal Stoa spanned the southern end. The Sanhedrin, the Jewish high court, had chambers here.

Herodian Temple Mount

First Temple Mount (Solomon)

Hasmonaean Extension (141 B.C.)

Wilson's Arch and bridge

Western Wall

Robinson's Arch

Preserved Herodian masonry

920 ft
280 m

1,590 ft
485 m

Temple Mount Cross Section

Temple

The Rock

Western Wall

SOUTH

Eastern wall

A.D. 691 | DOME OF THE ROCK

The octagonal masterpiece of the Dome of the Rock rose above Jerusalem in A.D. 691, followed soon by al-Aqsa Mosque. The rock came to be venerated as the spot from which Muhammad ascended to heaven during his mystical Night Journey from Mecca. Rubble of the Second Temple still remained when Muslims took the city from Christian Byzantine rulers in 638 and began to shape the complex into the Haram al-Sharif, the Noble Sanctuary, third holiest site in Islam.

Shown here as it would have looked in the early 700s, the Haram al-Sharif evolved in appearance and spiritual significance as the new faith of Islam grew. Muhammad had first taught his followers to pray facing the city where David, Solomon, and Jewish prophets had honored God.

Pool of the Sons of Israel

Gate of Mercy

Gate of the Tribes

HARAM AL-SHARIF

Ruins of the Temple Mount complex were gradually cleared as Muslims built new houses of worship.

DOME OF THE ROCK

Dome of the Chain

Gate of the Chain

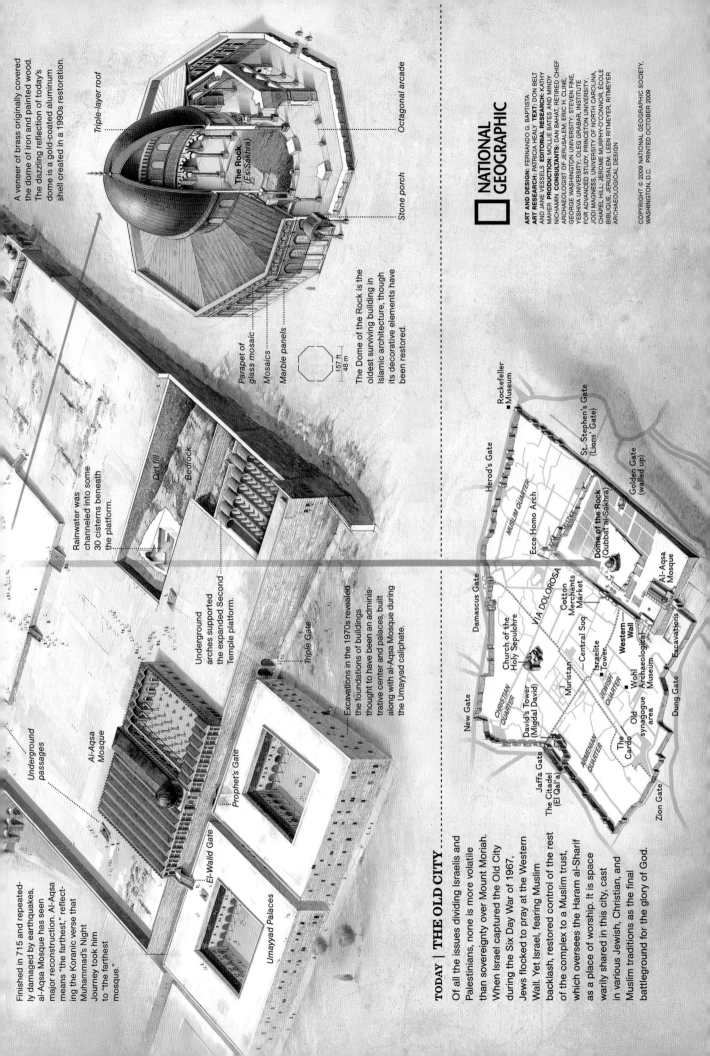

A veneer of brass originally covered the dome of iron and painted wood. The dazzling reflection of today's dome is a gold-coated aluminum shell created in a 1990s restoration.

Triple-layer roof

Octagonal arcade

The Rock (Es-Sakhra)

Stone porch

Parapet of glass mosaic

Mosaics

Marble panels

157 ft
48 m

The Dome of the Rock is the oldest surviving building in Islamic architecture, though its decorative elements have been restored.

Finished in 715 and repeatedly damaged by earthquakes, al-Aqsa Mosque has seen major reconstruction. Al-Aqsa means "the farthest," reflecting the Koranic verse that Muhammad's Night Journey took him to "the farthest mosque."

Underground passages

Al-Aqsa Mosque

Rainwater was channeled into some 30 cisterns beneath the platform.

Dirt fill

Bedrock

Underground arches supported the expanded Second Temple platform.

Triple Gate

Excavations in the 1970s revealed the foundations of buildings thought to have been an administrative center and palaces, built along with al-Aqsa Mosque during the Umayyad caliphate.

Prophet's Gate

El-Walid Gate

Umayyad Palaces

TODAY | THE OLD CITY

Of all the issues dividing Israelis and Palestinians, none is more volatile than sovereignty over Mount Moriah. When Israel captured the Old City during the Six Day War of 1967, Jews flocked to pray at the Western Wall. Yet Israel, fearing Muslim backlash, restored control of the rest of the complex to a Muslim trust, which oversees the Haram al-Sharif as a place of worship. It is space warily shared in this city, cast in various Jewish, Christian, and Muslim traditions as the final battleground for the glory of God.

Rockefeller Museum

Herod's Gate

St. Stephen's Gate (Lions' Gate)

Golden Gate (walled up)

MUSLIM QUARTER

Ecce Homo Arch

Dome of the Rock (Qubbat al-Sakhra)

Damascus Gate

VIA DOLOROSA

Church of the Holy Sepulchre

Cotton Merchants Market

Al-Aqsa Mosque

New Gate

CHRISTIAN QUARTER

David's Tower (Migdal David)

Muristan

Central Suq Market

Israelite Tower

Western Wall

Jaffa Gate

The Citadel (El Qal'a)

JEWISH QUARTER

Old synagogue area

Wohl Archaeological Museum

Excavations

The Cardo

Dung Gate

ARMENIAN QUARTER

Zion Gate

NATIONAL GEOGRAPHIC

ART AND DESIGN: FERNANDO G. BAPTISTA. ART RESEARCH: PATRICIA HEALY. TEXT: DON BELT AND JANE VESSELS EDITORIAL RESEARCH: KATHY MAHER PRODUCTION: MOLLIE BATES AND MINDY NICHAMIN. CONSULTANTS: DAN BAHAT, RETIRED CHIEF ARCHAEOLOGIST OF JERUSALEM; ERIC H. CLINE, GEORGE WASHINGTON UNIVERSITY; STEVEN FINE, YESHIVA UNIVERSITY; OLEG GRABAR, INSTITUTE FOR ADVANCED STUDY, PRINCETON UNIVERSITY; JODI MAGNESS, UNIVERSITY OF NORTH CAROLINA, CHAPEL HILL; JEROME MURPHY-O'CONNOR, ÉCOLE BIBLIQUE, JERUSALEM; LEEN RITMEYER, RITMEYER ARCHAEOLOGICAL DESIGN

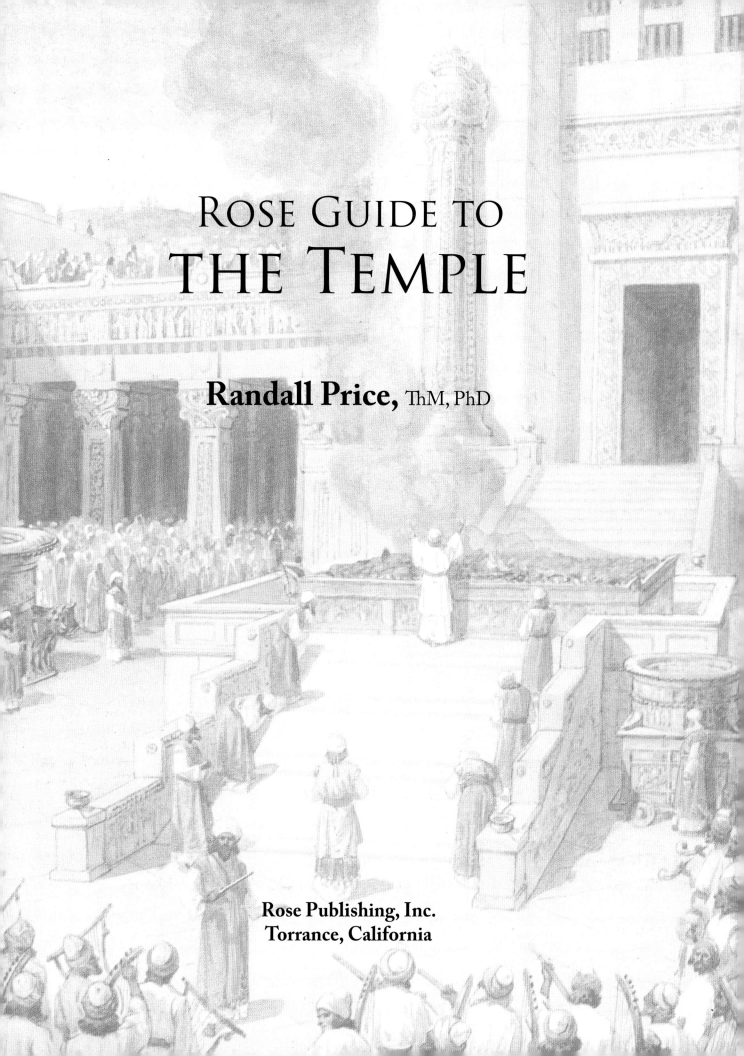

ROSE GUIDE TO
THE TEMPLE

Randall Price, ThM, PhD

Rose Publishing, Inc.
Torrance, California

Conditions of Use

Photographs, Illustrations and Other Credits

Author: Randall Price, ThM, PhD
Contributors: Aubrey Buster, MA; Shawn Vander Lugt, MA; Benjamín Galán, MTS, ThM
Illustrators: Cara Nilsen, caranilsen.blogspot.com; Stan Stein; Hugh Claycombe; Leen Ritmeyer, www.ritmeyer.com; Bill Latta; Balage Balogh, Archaeology Illustrated.com; Messiah in the Temple Foundation www.themessiahinthetemple.com, Foundation "Der Messias im Tempel" Basel, Switzerland; Alexander Schick/Uwe Beer www.bibelausstellung.de
Photo credits: Kim E. Walton, Walton Image Supply; Todd Bolen, BiblePlaces.com
Editor: Jessica Curiel, MA
Designer: Cristalle Kishi
Special thanks to Leen Ritmeyer for his comments and help with this project.

Library of Congress Cataloging-in-Publication Data

Price, Randall, 1951-
  Rose guide to the Temple / Randall Price.
    p. cm.
  Summary: "An archaeological exploration of the Temple Mount in Jerusalem from ancient times to modern day events. Diagrams, illustrations, maps, time lines, overlays and photographs trace God's sanctuary through the tabernacle, Solomon's Temple, Zerubbabel's Temple, Herod's Temple, the present Temple Mount, and the future temple"--Provided by publisher.
  Includes bibliographical references and index.
  ISBN 978-1-59636-468-4 (hardcover)
  1. Temple of Jerusalem (Jerusalem) I. Title.
  DS109.3.P75 2012
  296.4'91--dc23
                  2011039082

Printed by Oceanic Graphic International, Inc.
Printed in China
February 2014, 5th printing

CONTENTS

Section 3: God's Permanent Sanctuary Rebuilt: The Second Temple

Section 4: The Modern Temple Mount and Future Temple

Introduction

The temple built in Jerusalem is the most important building in history. Perhaps greater and grander structures have been built, but what makes the temple the most important is that God designed this structure as the place where his glorious presence would dwell. Though many times in history religions and political leaders have sought to deny, destroy, or replace the significance of the temple with shrines or symbols of their own, the temple and its site of the Temple Mount have continued even to this day to be before the eyes of the world.

- Christianity remembers the temple in association with the teachings of Jesus and the last week of his life on earth.

- Islamic tradition claims that a stone at the Temple Mount is the place where Abraham brought his son Ishmael and from which the prophet Muhammad ascended to heaven.

- Judaism, at least its Orthodox sect, still believes the divine presence attends the site. Most Orthodox Jews believe that the temple must one day be rebuilt.

These different perspectives on the temple have produced both controversy and conflict throughout history, and therefore those who would seek to understand the cause of this conflict must understand the subject of the temple itself.

Modern Jews and Christians often have difficulty understanding the concept of the temple and its sacrificial system. Although the temple was a familiar and accepted institution in early Judaism and the early church, its absence for the past 2,000 years has contributed to a lack of understanding regarding the temple's nature and importance. However, both Jews and Christians still utilize buildings in their worship of God and believe that his presence is in some way with them as they meet. If houses of worship are important for believers today, how much more necessary was the existence of a physical sanctuary when the divine presence visibly manifested itself with his people! Though the physical temple does not stand today, the spiritual sense of the sanctuary that we experience now should help us appreciate what God provided in the past.

> "One thing I ask from the Lord, this only do I seek: that I may dwell in the house of the Lord all the days of my life, to gaze on the beauty of the Lord and to seek him in his temple." —Psalm 27:4

It is therefore only fitting that this book presents the temple visually. God originally gave the temple to the people of Israel as a visual aid to comprehending God's glory in the heavenly temple and to show the way in which God in his holiness relates to people in their sinful condition. He provided its pattern by divine revelation and commanded that it be built according to his precise specifications. Every element in the design of the temple, like every garment and action of the priesthood, was intended for illustrating the divine ideal. From the beginning of creation, God communicated this divine ideal to humankind: He desires a relationship with his creatures, but on his terms, respecting his righteous standards.

Throughout the history of divine revelation, God has continued to express this divine ideal through the concept of a sanctuary, whether actual or symbolic. For this reason, we find the concept of sanctuary spanning the whole of written revelation—from the first book of the Old Testament to the last book of the New Testament. The more you are able to visualize this wonderful design, the greater you will enjoy this central teaching of the Word of God.

Although the Temple Mount today is the most *volatile* acreage on earth, for those who seek a relationship with the God of the universe, the study of the temple is one of the most *vital* activities for faith and worship. If you approach this study as one would approach the gates of the ancient temple with wonder and awe and then pass through with reverence, you will have the experience of the Israelites of old in gaining access to the knowledge of the Holy.

---⊶ SECTION 1 ⊶---
God's Sanctuary Before the Temple

OVERVIEW OF THE TEMPLE IN GOD'S PLAN

Creation and the Fall

The Bible reveals that God created humans in his image and that he desired from the beginning of creation to have a relationship with them (Genesis 1:26; 3:8). But when sin entered the world through the tragic event known as the Fall in the garden of Eden, humankind became alienated from God and forced God to exile them from his presence (Genesis 3:8–19, 23). To prevent them in this fallen state from reentering the garden, which represented a sanctuary where God's holiness had dwelt, God stationed cherubim to guard the entrance (Genesis 3:24).

Expulsion from the garden of Eden after the Fall

Sacrifices and Atonement

Yet God also revealed a way in which human sin could be forgiven and the broken relationship restored. God himself provided a substitute (an animal) whose blood (life) would atone for sin (Genesis 3:21). This began the sacrificial system. God also revealed the way in which he would return his presence to humanity and restore the earthly relationship once enjoyed in Eden; this was through the building of a sanctuary and maintaining a priesthood to serve God (Exodus 25:8; 27:21). First a tent-like structure called the tabernacle served as the sanctuary; it was later replaced by a permanent structure, the temple in Jerusalem. The sacrificial system was conducted within the tabernacle in the wilderness and later in the temple in Jerusalem (Deuteronomy 12:5–14).

David bringing the ark of the covenant to Jerusalem

God commanded that an ark of the covenant be constructed and topped with figures of cherubim like those once stationed outside the entrance to Eden (Exodus 25:10; 18–20). This ark was placed in the holiest room of the tabernacle and later the temple. This revealed that once atonement had been made it was again possible for humankind to enter God's presence which was manifested at the ark. However, this was done only through a mediator, the high priest, who represented God's people (Exodus 28:12, 29). The sacrifices and the atonement conducted by the priests of Israel foreshadowed a coming sacrifice and a high priest who would make atonement once for all.

Jesus

When Jesus came to earth as Messiah, much of his teaching and ministry took place at the temple. He was dedicated at the temple as an infant (Luke 2:27); he brought sacrifices from his home in Galilee three times a year to the temple (Luke 2:41–42); he often taught in the temple precincts (John 18:20); he called the temple "my father's house" (Luke 2:49; John 2:16); and he showed great zeal for it as a holy sanctuary (John 2:17; see also Psalm 69:9). At the moment Jesus died on the cross, the temple veil was torn in two from top to bottom (Mark 15:38). With his death on the cross, Christ who was sinless became the perfect sacrifice for sin (Ephesians 5:2). He laid down his life willingly and became not only the sacrifice, but also the one who offers the sacrifice—the ultimate high priest (Hebrews 5:6–10; 7:24). The author of Hebrews writes, "…we have confidence to enter the Most Holy Place by the blood of Jesus, by a new and living way opened for us through the curtain, that is, his body, and since we have a great priest over the house of God, let us draw near to God with a sincere heart" (Hebrews 10:19–22).

The Church

After Jesus' resurrection and ascension into heaven, the apostles and the early church continued to worship at the temple (Luke 24:53; Acts 2:46; 3:1). The apostle Paul uses the sanctity of the temple to teach that the bodies of believers as the church itself is holy because God's presence (as the Holy Spirit) dwells there, and therefore it must not be defiled by sinful acts (Ephesians 2:21–22; 1 Corinthians 3:16-17; 6:19–20; 2 Corinthians 6:16–17). Paul likewise states that believers are "sanctified," have a calling as "saints" and have a "spiritual service"—all language borrowed from the temple and its priesthood (1 Corinthians 1:2; Romans 12:2; 1 Peter 2:9).

Christ's sacrifice for us on the cross

The New Jerusalem

The book of Revelation points all believers to their hope in a future heavenly home of the saints—the New Jerusalem. This will be a place whose very structure mirrors the temple's inner sanctuary, the Holy of Holies, where God's presence dwells (Revelation 21). This final image reminds us that all of the things related to the temple on earth were but copies of the things already eternal in the heavens, and that God's purpose in bringing the temple into existence was to bring a bit of heaven to earth. As we keep in mind these great truths, we will increasingly see the abounding riches of God manifested in the design and duties of the temple and its priesthood, and understand the lessons God intends for us.

The Temple Before Time

The Bible, both in the Old and New Testaments, speaks of a heavenly temple which served as the abode of God and as the pattern for the construction of the earthly tabernacle and temples. The heavenly temple is the place where God dwells, where one can seek his counsel, and the place from where he sends divine revelation.

OLD TESTAMENT	NEW TESTAMENT
• Moses, Aaron and his sons, and 70 of the elders of Israel saw a glimpse of the heavenly temple (Exodus 24:9–10). • David may have referred to the heavenly temple in the Psalms (Psalms 11:4; 23:6; 27:4–6; 138:2). • During the reign of the Israelite king, Ahab, a prophet named Micaiah saw the heavenly temple (1 Kings 22:19), as did the prophet Isaiah after entering the earthly temple to seek the Lord upon the death of the Judean king, Uzziah (Isaiah 6:1–5). • The prophet Ezekiel, while in exile in Babylon, saw a vision of the Lord enthroned in the heavenly temple (Ezekiel 1:1–28).	• The book of Hebrews draws a distinction between the "earthly sanctuary" and a "greater and more perfect tabernacle, not made with hands, that is to say, not of this creation" (Hebrews 9:1, 11). This place is located in "heaven itself … in the presence of God" (verse 24). It is the place where one can find holy, heavenly vessels and where Christ serves as High Priest (verses 21–25). • In the book of Revelation, the heavenly temple appears as the place where the apostle John receives revelation (Revelation 7:15; 14:17; 16:17). "After this I looked, and I saw in heaven the temple—that is, the tabernacle of the covenant law—and it was opened" (15:5).

Many scholars believe that the earthly sanctuaries, like the tabernacle and the temple, were constructed to bring a sense of the heavenly temple to the earthly realm in order for God to dwell among humankind. The earthly tabernacle and temples were constructed from a divine design given by divine revelation to Moses (Exodus 25:8–9, 40) and King David (1 Chronicles 28:11–19). The earthly sanctuaries became an institution which made it possible for humans to commune with God to a limited capacity.

The author of the book of Hebrews encourages believers to look forward to a time when they will dwell in a heavenly city (Hebrews 13:14). Abraham is described as one who was "looking for the city which has foundations, whose architect and builder is God … a better country, that is a heavenly one" (Hebrews 11:10, 16). The book of Revelation identifies this city as the New Jerusalem—a city "laid out as a square" forming a cube 1,500 miles (2,414 kilometers) on each side. At first glance, it appears that the New Jerusalem doesn't contain a temple because John doesn't see one in his vision (Revelation 21:22). However, since the Holy of Holies bears a strong resemblance (in a much-condensed form) to the cube-shaped city, some scholars suggest that the New Jerusalem is actually the Holy of Holies—the throne room—of the heavenly temple. The New Jerusalem doesn't *contain* a temple; the New Jerusalem *is* the Holy of Holies of the heavenly temple.

With the descent of the New Jerusalem to earth (or just above the earth), Revelation 21:3 announces that the "tabernacle of God is among men, and He will dwell among them, and they shall be His people, and God Himself will be among them" (NASB). It is here, within this holy city, where the complete reconciliation between God and humankind will occur. Forever, humans and God will exist together in an unlimited relationship. The earthly temples were symbols of the presence of God with his people, but at the same time, they were mere copies of the heavenly temple, which is the presence of God.

PRE-TEMPLE SANCTUARIES

The Garden of Eden

A number of clues in the book of Genesis reveal that God created the garden of Eden as a pre-temple sanctuary for his presence.[1] The garden and the tabernacle/temple share a similar physical arrangement. In Genesis, God planted the garden "toward the east, in Eden" (Genesis 2:8 NASV). Later we read that God stationed cherubim at "the east of the garden of Eden" to prevent anyone from returning west to the Tree of Life (Genesis 3:24). In the book of Numbers, this east-west orientation is the basis for the tribal arrangement for Moses, Aaron, and his sons who perform the service of the tabernacle (Numbers 3:38).

Certain sacred objects also appear in the garden and the tabernacle/temple. The sacred Tree of Life in the center of the garden can be compared to the sacred candelabra (menorah) in the central section of the Holy Place. The two cherubim posted at the east entrance to Eden (Genesis 3:24) can be compared to the two cherubim overshadowing the mercy seat on the ark of the covenant (Exodus 25:18–22), embroidered on the veil of the tabernacle (Exodus 26:31), and carved into the walls, doors, and paneling of the first temple (1 Kings 6:27–35; 7:29, 36).

The duties of Adam in the garden also suggest a sanctuary existed because his responsibility was to "work" and "keep" (Genesis 2:15). These terms, used elsewhere only of the Levites who served in the tabernacle and temple, suggest that Adam had been commissioned to act as a "priest of God" preserving and protecting the holy ground of the garden-sanctuary.

When the tabernacle was constructed, God's presence there depended upon his peoples' obedience to the laws of the tabernacle (Leviticus 26:1–46). In the same way, God's presence in the garden depended upon obedience to the one law of respecting the Tree of the Knowledge of Good and Evil (Genesis 2:17; 3:1–3). In Genesis, this exile was from the garden sanctuary (Genesis 3:23–24). For Israel, disobedience meant exile from the presence of God, the destruction of the temple, and exile from the Promised Land.

The arrangement of the garden's landscape corresponds to the arrangement of the tabernacle and temple's furniture. Eastward movement (out of the garden) is away from God's presence; westward movement (through the garden) is a return of God. On the Day of Atonement, the high priest moved through the sanctuary closer to the presence of God symbolizing the people's reversal of spiritual exile from God. For these reasons, it appears that God showed the divine design for the temple at the beginning of history and that later constructions of buildings followed this pattern.

When we compare the garden sanctuary to the tabernacle we discover an important difference.

The Garden of Eden

Garden of Eden

Presence of God

Tree of Life

The Fall (Exile) Eastward

Tree of the Knowledge of Good and Evil

Flaming Sword

Mountain of the Lord

Cherubim

Euphrates   Tigris   Gihon   Pison

Tabernacle

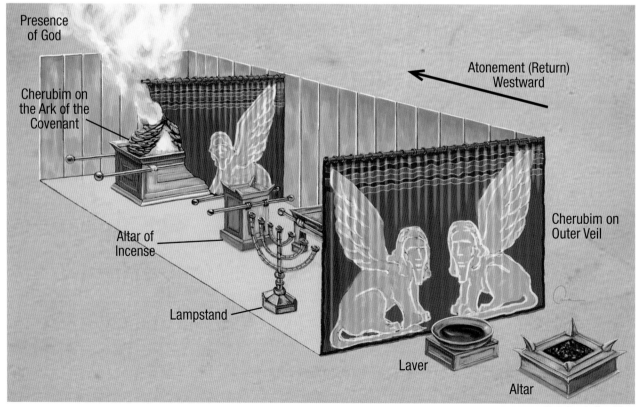

Presence of God

Atonement (Return) Westward

Cherubim on the Ark of the Covenant

Altar of Incense

Lampstand

Cherubim on Outer Veil

Laver

Altar

Illustrations by Cara Nilsen

TENT OF MEETING

During the time of the tabernacle's construction, Moses built a "tent of meeting" outside the camp so he could privately enter into God's presence (the *shekinah*) and receive divine guidance and answers to the people's prayers (Exodus 33:7–11). This tent seems to have been a provisional structure that was later incorporated into the tabernacle, since the terms *tent of meeting* and *tabernacle* are used interchangeably after the tabernacle's completion (Lev. 1:3; Deut. 31:14–15). God moved about "in a tent, even in a tabernacle" (2 Sam. 7:6). Years later when the first temple was dedicated by Solomon, the portable tent of meeting/tabernacle and its sacred vessels were incorporated into the temple (1 Kings 8:4).

The cherubim stationed at the entrance to God's presence in Eden faced *outward*, preventing people from re-entering the sacred site. However, in the Holy of Holies, the cherubim were positioned on top of the mercy seat of the ark with their faces turned *inward* toward God's presence. These cherubim, rather than turning people away from God's presence, made it possible for the high priest as a mediator to enter God's presence (Exodus 25:8, 22). The first man, Adam, served as a representative for humankind and caused exile from God's presence. The high priest served as a representative for Israel enabling God's people to reenter God's presence. God's command to build him a sanctuary was the gracious means by which he brought humanity back into a relationship with him (Exodus 25:8).

The Tabernacle: God's Sanctuary in Motion

After God brought his people out of slavery in Egypt, God revealed to Moses on Mt. Sinai the divine design for the tabernacle (Exodus 25:2, 8–9, 40; Hebrews 8:5; 9:24). The tabernacle was a collapsible building that the Israelites transported through the wilderness and later during the period of settlement in the Promised Land.

This tabernacle served God's purpose as a sanctuary for 485 years (from Moses to Solomon). Its purpose was to make possible God's dwelling with his people (Exodus 25:8). It was made to be an earthly copy of the heavenly sanctuary. Because of sin, God could not physically coexist with humans (Exodus 33:20; Isaiah 59:2). Dwelling with God was only possible if there was a proper separation (the curtains of the tabernacle), a sanctified place of meeting (the ark of the covenant within the Holy of Holies), and a qualified mediator (the high priest).

The details of this structure and the rules of ritual purification that maintained its sanctity were carefully described to Moses and two craftsmen: Bezalel and Oholiab. These men were divinely appointed to supervise skilled workers in making the structural framework, tent curtains, and ritual furniture of the tabernacle (Exodus 25:10–40:33). In addition, God instructed the priests how to conduct the divine service and how to prevent ritual desecration. Also, the people were told how to live godly lives that would sustain them collectively as a priestly nation (Exodus 20:24–25:9). The materials for the tabernacle's construction came from the voluntary contributions of the people who had received these costly items of metals, skins, and fabrics as part of the "plunder from the Egyptians" (Exodus 3:22; 12:35–36; 25:2–7).

The tabernacle was situated in the middle of the twelve tribes of Israel (Numbers 2:17; 10:14–28). This location for the tabernacle was necessary because it served as the focal point of Israel's daily life. In this way, God, whose presence was manifested at the tabernacle as a cloud by day and a pillar of fire by night, was continually at the center of his people (Exodus 33:9–10; Numbers 14:14).

The Tabernacle Cutaway

THREE PARTS OF THE TABERNACLE

The tabernacle had three main sections. Each section contained special, sacred objects. Each section was also the place of different sacred activities.

The Courtyard

The Courtyard was the main access to the tabernacle. The wide gate was the place where ancient Israelites would bring their sacrifices and offerings. There, the priests would receive and bless people. Within the courtyard, the priests would offer sacrifices at the bronze altar. There was also a bronze laver, in which the priests could cleanse themselves to be ritually clean.

The Holy Place

The Holy Place housed three important objects for the service of the tabernacle: the golden lamp, the table of the bread of the presence, and the altar of incense. The priests performed daily tasks inside the Holy Place: they had to keep the lamps burning, offer incense twice a day, and bring fresh bread weekly to the table.

The Holy of Holies (Most Holy Place)

The Holy of Holies was a unique place. The ark of the covenant was in this room. God's very presence dwelt in the Holy of Holies. Only the high priest could enter this room once a year, protected by a cloud of smoke from burnt incense. The most important celebration in the Jewish calendar, the Day of Atonement, had its climax in the Holy of Holies, where the high priest offered the blood of the sacrificed animal to God to atone for the people's sin.

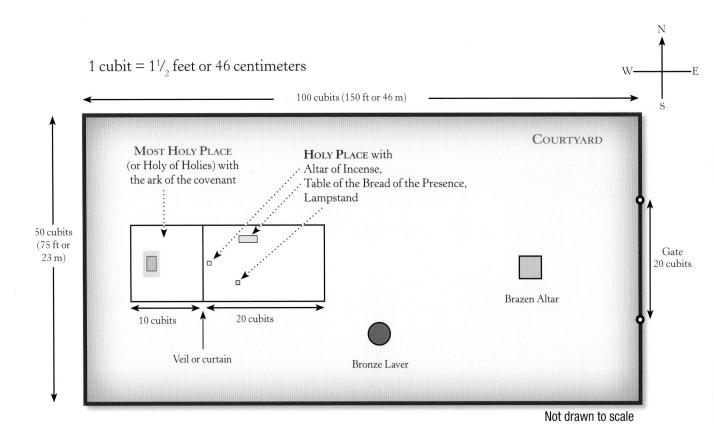

1 cubit = 1½ feet or 46 centimeters

100 cubits (150 ft or 46 m)

50 cubits (75 ft or 23 m)

MOST HOLY PLACE (or Holy of Holies) with the ark of the covenant

HOLY PLACE with Altar of Incense, Table of the Bread of the Presence, Lampstand

COURTYARD

Gate 20 cubits

Brazen Altar

10 cubits   20 cubits

Veil or curtain

Bronze Laver

Not drawn to scale

WHAT DOES "TEMPLE" MEAN?

The English word "temple" comes from the Latin *templum*, following the Greek *temenos*, which refers to a raised platform often dedicated to a sacred purpose. However, the Greek and Hebrew words used to refer to the "temple" in Scripture provide a complete understanding of this term.

Old Testament

The earliest form of the sanctuary, the tabernacle, was called in Hebrew *mishkan* ("dwelling"). The Hebrew term *hekal* is probably derived from Sumerian *e-gal* meaning "big house." The nonspecific sense of this term is of a "palace" or a "shrine," and it may refer generally to any ancient Near Eastern center of worship. The more specific use was of God's special "house," the Jerusalem temple (2 Kings 18:16; Jeremiah 7:4). The Bible most often calls the temple *Beit YHWH* (the "house of the LORD") or *Beit 'Elohim* (the "house of God") which refers to the temple as a place where God's presence resides.

Another Hebrew word, *miqdash* ("holy place"), usually translated as "sanctuary," was used to refer to the tent of meeting and the *sancta* (vessels and priestly personnel). Sometimes the word *miqdash* is used of the Holy of Holies (Leviticus 16:33), the tabernacle compound (Leviticus 19:30), and the temple precinct (Ezekiel 43:21). On occasion, it was used of rival Israelite temples both inside and outside the land (Amos 7:9, 13), but most often it referred to the one legitimate sanctuary—the temple in Jerusalem (Isaiah 63:18). Modern Hebrew uses this word when it refers to the ancient temples as *Beit Hamikdash*.

The Greek version of the Hebrew Bible, known as the Septuagint (LXX), followed the Hebrew use of *mishkan* with its term *naos*, a noun derived from the verb *naio* ("to dwell" or "inhabit") and *miqdash* ("sanctuary"). In Classical Greek, *naos* referred to the "abode of the gods," with specific reference to the innermost part of a shrine, which contained the image of a god. However, the Septuagint uses this word 55 out of 61 times to translate the Hebrew *hekal*. Had the Septuagint intended "*a* temple" in general, it might have used the Greek term *heiron* ("sacred edifice") to translate *hekal*. However, the predominate usage of *naos* to refer to the "temple of God" in Jerusalem implies it understood *hekal* with this technical meaning.

New Testament

In the New Testament, the Greek word *naos* is used to refer to the inner part of the temple (the Holy of Holies) in distinction to the outer part of the temple (the temple precinct). This distinction is important for understanding Jesus' pronouncement in Luke 21:6 about the buildings of the temple: "the days will come in which there will not be left one stone upon another which will not be torn down" (NASB). Since the retaining walls of the temple precinct remain standing even today, how can it be said that "not one stone would be left that would not be torn down"? The answer is that Jesus was referring to the buildings of the *naos* (the temple proper) and not to those of the *heiron* (the outer precincts, which would include the retaining walls). All of the buildings in the temple proper were indeed completely destroyed.

Because *naos* had a particular reference to the part of the temple where the *shekinah* (God's presence) dwelt, the apostle Paul used that word to refer to the spiritual indwelling of the Holy Spirit in believers. This special relationship made it possible to make a spiritual application to the believer's body as a "temple" (1 Corinthians 3:16–17; 6:19) and to the church as a spiritual "temple" (Ephesians 2:21–22). It also allowed Christians to be called "saints" (*hagaoi*, literally "holy ones") and to refer to their "spiritual worship" as a "priestly service" (see Romans 12:1 where the Greek term *latreuō* is used regularly in the LXX to "rendering priestly service," cf. Romans 15:16).

HOW DO WE KNOW ABOUT THE TEMPLE?

Fortunately, the ancient world has left us with a wealth of information about the ancient temple. We would, of course, like to have had certain details reconciled and explained, but we are grateful that we have the details necessary to reconstruct the various designs of the temple through time and to understand how they were used. There has also been many legends and fanciful stories about the temple, therefore, it is important to know the best sources for reliable information. The three main sources are written documents, archaeological excavations, and architectural investigations. These sources have enabled scholars to reconstruct models of the first and second temples, as well as the temple envisioned by the prophet Ezekiel.

Written Documents

The written document we are most familiar with is the Bible which records details of God's instruction for the temple's construction and role in the covenants God made with Israel. Other major written documents are the works of the first-century Jewish historian Flavius Josephus and the writings of the rabbis. We also have important information provided by some Greek, Roman, and Christian sources.

RABBINIC WRITING	DESCRIPTION
Mishnah	This is the oldest comprehensive systematic-theological exposition of the Jewish Law which consists of a collection of 4,187 rules of dogma written down by Rabbi Yehuda Ha-Nasi in the second century AD.
Gemara	This is a collection of later rabbinical discussions about the Mishnah. *Gemara* means "completion."
Talmud	This is the most significant theological work of post-biblical Judaism compiled between AD 200–600. It contains additional discussion on the temple and its priestly activities. It exists in two editions: one from Babylon and one from Jerusalem; these contain the same Mishnah, but different Gemara.

One problem in consulting these rabbinic writings is that they are often incomplete. For example, the rabbis who lived at the time of Jesus did not comment in their writings on the additions that King Herod—the hated puppet king set up by the Romans—made to the Temple Mount.

A second problem is that these sources seem to offer contradictory measurements of the second temple. For example, Josephus says that the east portico (covered porch) of the second temple was 400 cubits long,[2] but the Mishnah states that the Temple Mount was 500 cubits square. [3]

FLAVIUS JOSEPHUS
(AD 37–101)

Josephus was from a priestly family and understood the form and function of the temple. He grew up during the last decades of the second temple and provides a firsthand account of its appearance at that time. He also witnessed or had firsthand acquaintance with both Jews and Romans who were part of its destruction in AD 70. His works that record the details of the temple are *Antiquities of the Jews* and *War of the Jews*. Josephus eventually became a Roman citizen commissioned to write Jewish history for a Roman audience. History and archaeology have proved the accuracy of his accounts regarding the temple in even the smallest details.

Archaeology

Archaeological excavation and architectural investigations have also contributed much to verifying the details in the literary sources and providing new information. However, due to religious and political sensitivity of the Temple Mount, only limited exploration directly on the site has been allowed since the nineteenth century. After the Israeli victory in the Six-Day War in 1967 in which Israel gained control of East Jerusalem, Israeli archaeologists have had access to some remains of the temple complex, but excavation has only taken place outside the great retaining walls of the Temple Mount.

Beginning in 1996, the Islamic authorities removed more than 20,000 tons of archaeologically rich debris from the southern and eastern portions of the Temple Mount in preparation for the construction of the Al-Marwani Mosque. This material was dumped into the Kidron Valley. The Temple Mount Sifting Project is a means of searching through this rubble and salvaging what evidence could be found of a Jewish presence on the Temple Mount. To date, tons of pottery have been salvaged, half of which is dated to the first and second temple periods.

Excavated temples in the ancient Near East, particularly the temple of 'Ain Dara in Syria, contain many similarities to the temple in Jerusalem, making it possible for archaeologists to reconstruct a portrait of the temple built by Solomon. In recent years, the discovery and excavation of the Samaritan temple on Mt. Gerizim (in modern-day West Bank) has provided unique insights into the structure of the earlier second temple and its complex. Other archaeological discoveries have provided information through inscriptions and artifacts related to the temple and its priesthood.

Temple Mount Sifting Project

(Above photo courtesy of Alexander Schick ©www.bibelausstellung.de)

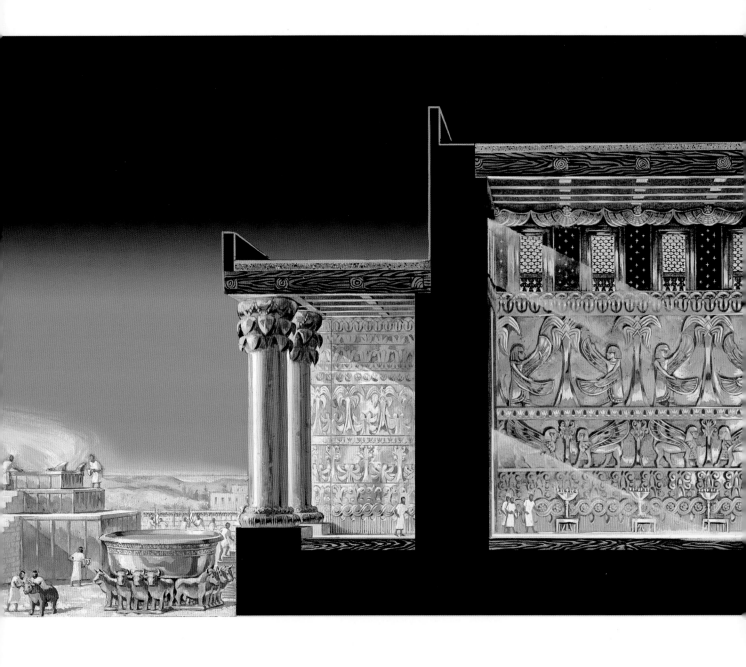

— ∘ SECTION 2 ∘ —

God's Permanent Sanctuary: The First Temple

BUILDING THE FIRST TEMPLE

It may seem odd that the building of the first temple waited so many centuries after God's people entered into the Promised Land, but God had a particular order of events that was necessary to prepare for this event. This preparation involved the boundaries of the Promised Land coming under Israelite control, the enemies of the people being subdued, and the proper individuals coming onto the stage of history to perform the work.

The Divine Source: Directions for the "House of the Lord"

After Moses had brought the children of Israel through the sea, his first statement about God's plans for the people was, "You will bring them in and plant them on the mountain of your inheritance—the place, LORD, you

David Brings the Ark to Jerusalem. In this painting, King David wears an ephod and leads the Kohathite priests bearing the ark of the covenant from the house of Obed-edom (a gatekeeper for the ark) to Jerusalem (2 Samuel 6:12; 1 Chronicles 15:25). The artist has taken some liberties with the canopy over the ark as well as the cloth directly covering it, which was actually blue in color, as was the covering for all of the sacred vessels within the tabernacle (see Numbers 4:5–12). (Painting by William Brassey Hole)

made for your dwelling, the sanctuary, Lord, your hands established" (Exodus 15:17). God instructed Moses that once Israel crossed into the Promised Land they were to establish a central sanctuary in "the place that the LORD your God shall choose" (Deut. 12:10–18). However, they wouldn't set up God's permanent sanctuary until God had given them rest from their enemies so they would live in safety.

Many years later, a man from Bethlehem named David was crowned king of Israel and reigned in Hebron, a city about 20 miles (32 kilometers) southwest of Jerusalem. After reigning in Hebron for seven years and six months, David and his army attacked the Jebusites who lived in Jerusalem. The Jebusites didn't think David's army would be successful, but to their dismay, David and his men captured Jerusalem. David set up residence in the fortress of Zion and called it the City of David. Hiram, the king of Tyre, built a magnificent palace for David and David became powerful because God was with him.

For 20 years the ark of the covenant had been kept in the house of a resident at Kiriath-Jerarim, a city about 10 miles (16 km) outside of Jerusalem. After David established himself in Jerusalem, he gathered up his army and moved the ark from Kiriath-Jerarim to Jerusalem. David pitched a tent in Jerusalem and placed the ark inside. Unfortunately, David continued to face conflicts with surrounding nations, especially the Philistines.

> *"Then Solomon began to build the temple of the LORD in Jerusalem on Mount Moriah, where the LORD had appeared to his father David. It was on the threshing floor of Araunah the Jebusite, the place provided by David."*
> —2 Chronicles 3:1

As David sat in his palace, he contemplated building a permanent sanctuary for the Lord. He felt guilty that he himself lived in "a house of cedar, while the ark of the covenant of the LORD is under a tent" (1 Chronicles 17:1). After consulting the Lord, the prophet Nathan told David that David's son would build the temple. God promised David that he would expand his kingdom and remove all of David's enemies. God also promised David that his descendants would always sit on the throne of Israel.

Later in his life, David sinned against God and God sent a plague upon Israel as judgment. David confessed and the prophet Gad instructed David to purchase a threshing floor that belonged to Araunah the Jebusite. David purchased the threshing floor, built an altar, and sacrificed offerings to God. When God answered with fire from heaven, David was convinced that "the house of the Lord God" needed to be built upon that site (1 Chronicles 22:1).

In the time of Abraham and Isaac, God gave the general location for the sanctuary in the Promised Land with the altar Abraham built on Mt. Moriah and with God's provision for a substitutionary sacrifice at that spot (Genesis 22:2, 13–14). Then, in David's time, God identified the site even more specifically as the threshing floor of Araunah the Jebusite on Mt. Moriah in Jerusalem (1 Chronicles 21:18–20).

Although David was "a man after [God's] own heart" (1 Samuel 13:14) and "David had it in his heart to build a temple for the Name of the Lord, the God of Israel" (2 Chronicles 6:7–8), God did not permit David to build the temple because of the warfare in his day (1 Kings 5:3; 8:18–19; 1 Chronicles 28:3–4). David knew that his son Solomon was young and inexperienced, so he wanted to provide Solomon with the wisdom and materials needed to build the temple (1 Chronicles 22:5). God revealed the design plans for the first temple in the same manner in which Moses had received the plan for the tabernacle on Mt. Sinai. King David then communicated the details of the plan for the temple and all its furnishings to his son Solomon (1 Chronicles 28:11–19).

David Buys the Threshing Floor. In this painting, King David purchases the threshing floor of Araunah (Ornan) the Jebusite on Mt. Moriah (2 Samuel 24:18–25). This was the site where the Angel of the Lord had stood to destroy Jerusalem, but was restrained by God's command (1 Chronicles 21:15). In the sky (upper right), the artist has given us a glimpse of this angel who has lingered to observe this historic purchase. On this site David built an altar to the Lord, establishing it as the place for the first and second temples (2 Chronicles 3:1; Ezra 6:7).

(Painting by William Brassey Hole)

Jerusalem Through the Years

Modern-day Jerusalem is a sprawling metropolis, but back in David's time, it was only a few acres in size. These diagrams show how Jerusalem grew. Notice the comparison between the Old City walls today and the size of Jerusalem at that time.

Black indicates the present walls of Old City Jerusalem.

Yellow indicates the size of Jerusalem at that time.

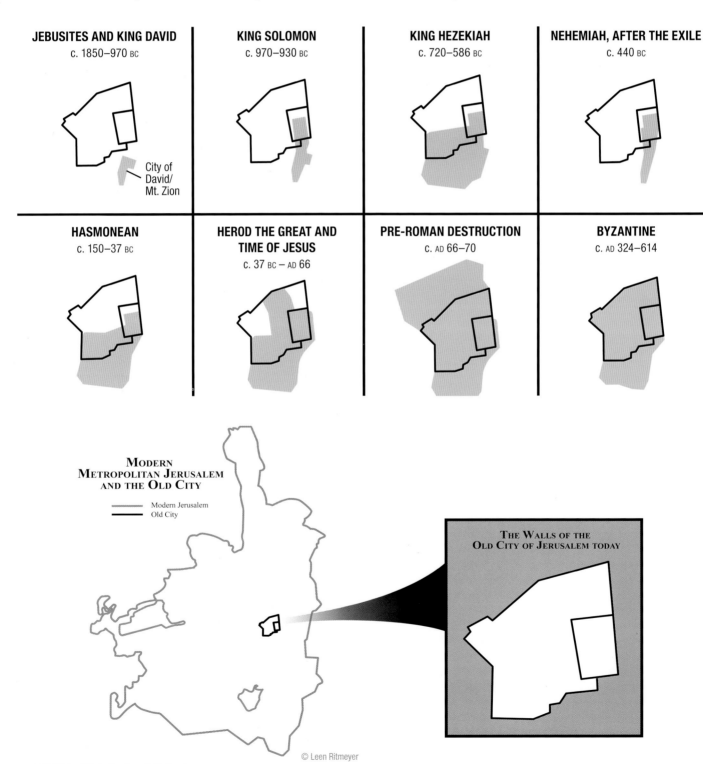

JEBUSITES AND KING DAVID
c. 1850–970 BC

City of David/ Mt. Zion

KING SOLOMON
c. 970–930 BC

KING HEZEKIAH
c. 720–586 BC

NEHEMIAH, AFTER THE EXILE
c. 440 BC

HASMONEAN
c. 150–37 BC

HEROD THE GREAT AND TIME OF JESUS
c. 37 BC – AD 66

PRE-ROMAN DESTRUCTION
c. AD 66–70

BYZANTINE
c. AD 324–614

MODERN
METROPOLITAN JERUSALEM
AND THE OLD CITY

—— Modern Jerusalem
—— Old City

THE WALLS OF THE
OLD CITY OF JERUSALEM TODAY

© Leen Ritmeyer

The Holy Land

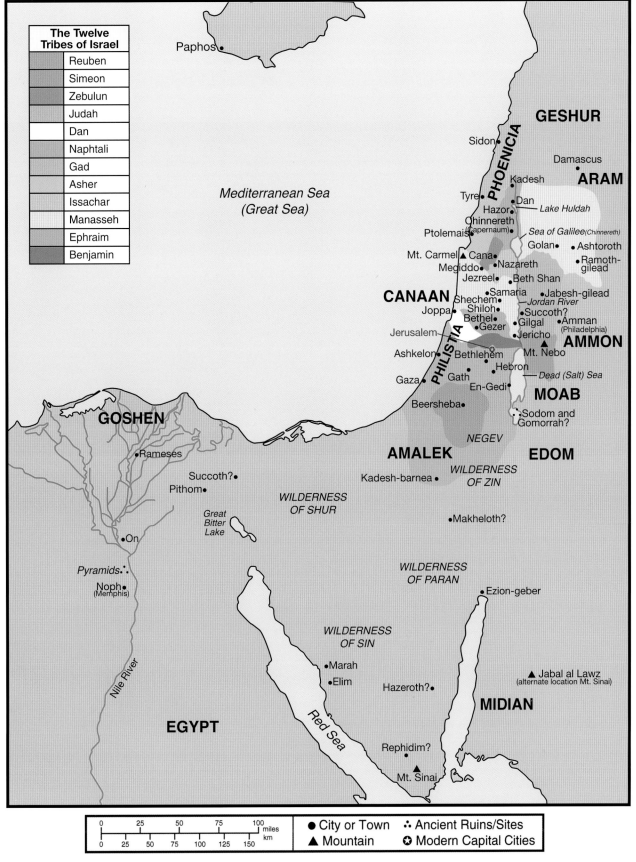

The Twelve Tribes of Israel

- Reuben
- Simeon
- Zebulun
- Judah
- Dan
- Naphtali
- Gad
- Asher
- Issachar
- Manasseh
- Ephraim
- Benjamin

Paphos

Mediterranean Sea
(Great Sea)

GESHUR

Sidon
PHOENICIA
Damascus
ARAM
Kadesh
Tyre
Hazor
Dan Lake Huldah
Chinnereth
(Capernaum)
Ptolemais
Sea of Galilee (Chinnereth)
Golan Ashtoroth
Mt. Carmel Cana
Ramoth-gilead
Megiddo Nazareth
Jezreel Beth Shan
CANAAN Samaria Jabesh-gilead
Shechem Jordan River
Joppa Shiloh Succoth?
Bethel Amman
Jerusalem Gezer Gilgal (Philadelphia)
PHILISTIA Jericho AMMON
Ashkelon Bethlehem Mt. Nebo
Gaza Gath Hebron Dead (Salt) Sea
En-Gedi MOAB
Beersheba Sodom and
Gomorrah?
NEGEV
AMALEK EDOM
WILDERNESS
Kadesh-barnea OF ZIN

GOSHEN

Rameses

Succoth?
Pithom
WILDERNESS
OF SHUR
Makheloth?

Great
Bitter
Lake

On

Pyramids
WILDERNESS
OF PARAN
Noph
(Memphis)
Ezion-geber

WILDERNESS
OF SIN
Marah
Elim
Jabal al Lawz
(alternate location Mt. Sinai)
Hazeroth?

Nile River

MIDIAN

EGYPT
Red Sea
Rephidim?

Mt. Sinai

| 0 | 25 | 50 | 75 | 100 miles |
| 0 | 25 | 50 | 75 | 100 | 125 | 150 km |

● City or Town ∴ Ancient Ruins/Sites
▲ Mountain ✪ Modern Capital Cities

The Human Source: The Construction Budget and Crew

The building of the temple was assigned to David's son Solomon whose name means "his peace," indicating that the temple was to be constructed in a time of peace by a man of peace. However, David was permitted to make preparations for his son. As with the preparations for the tabernacle, preparations for the temple were done through raising the necessary financial contributions from the people. The tribal leaders of Israel contributed generously, and David as well gave much from his own royal treasury. Together David and the people donated gold, refined silver, bronze, iron, and numerous precious stones (1 Chronicles 29:1–9).

	DAVID'S ROYAL TREASURY	LEADERS OF ISRAEL	TOTAL
Gold	100 tons	170 tons	270 tons
Silver	235 tons	340 tons	575 tons
Bronze	–	610 tons	610 tons
Iron	–	3,400 tons	3,400 tons

(Weights approximate; based on the metric ton)

When King Solomon assumed the task of construction, he knew a massive crew would be needed to fulfill his seven-year building plan.

- Solomon contracted with King Hiram of Tyre to furnish the building materials and skilled craftsmen to complete the job. (Tyre was an ancient Phoenician port city in Lebanon.)

- Solomon bartered for Sidonian woodsmen to cut timber in Lebanon and transport the lumber to Joppa (1 Kings 5:6–9).

- Solomon employed 70,000 porters and 80,000 stonecutters who worked in the mountains under 3,600 supervisors (2 Chronicles 2:18).

- Phoenician and Gebalite stonemasons quarried the large stones for the foundation of the temple as well as the dressed stones for the building (1 Kings 5:18).

- Solomon acquired a skilled craftsman named Huram-Abi. Huram was skilled in bronze, gold, silver, iron, wood, and stone—as well as yarn and fine linen.

- Solomon also drafted forced laborers from among the 12 tribes of Israel totalling about 30,000 (1 Kings 5:13; 2 Chronicles 2:2).

If sold on the market today, the 575 tons of silver would go for about $755 million US dollars. The 270 tons of gold would be worth an astounding $15.3 billion dollars!

Plan and Section of Solomon's Temple

Solomon's temple faced east. In front of the temple was the porch, supported by two bronze pillars, Yachin ("He [God] will establish") and Boaz ("In him [God] is strength"). The sanctuary itself consisted of the Holy Place, which measured 40 cubits (60 ft; 18 m) by 20 cubits (30 ft; 9 m), while the Holy of Holies was a cube of 20 cubits (30 ft; 9 m). There were three levels of side chambers built around the sanctuary, which had ledges in the outer wall to support the floors. These chambers were used for storing the temple treasuries.

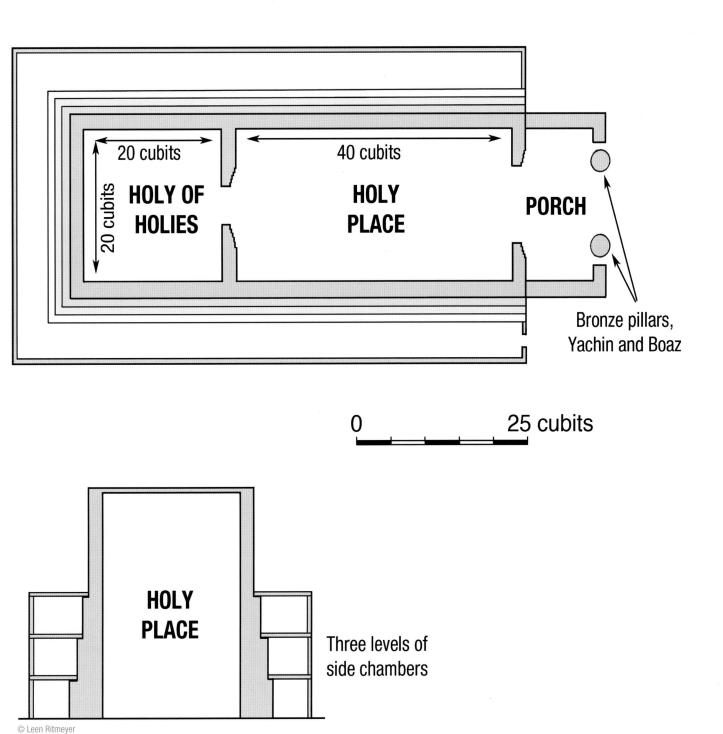

20 cubits

20 cubits

HOLY OF HOLIES

40 cubits

HOLY PLACE

PORCH

Bronze pillars, Yachin and Boaz

0   25 cubits

HOLY PLACE

Three levels of side chambers

© Leen Ritmeyer

Solomon's Dedication of the Temple.
In this painting of the dedication of the first temple
(1 Kings 8; 2 Chronicles 2), the Levitical priests are
in the foreground with musical instruments while the
Zadokite priests carry incense. The high priest offers a
burnt offering on the brazen altar before the entrance
to the temple flanked by the massive bronze pillars of
Yachin and Boaz. These pillars are depicted as free-
standing, however archaeologists now believe they
were load-bearing structures and therefore part of the
entrance porch. (Painting by William Brassey Hole)

Solomon's Dedication of the Temple

The temple was completed in 960 BC after seven years of construction. "When all the work King Solomon had done for the temple of the LORD was finished, he brought in the things his father David had dedicated— the silver and gold and the furnishings—and he placed them in the treasuries of the LORD's temple" (1 Kings 7:51). The priests brought the ark of the covenant into the Holy of Holies and set it under the wings of the cherubim. Then the Lord's presence filled the temple and Solomon blessed everyone watching. He announced that God would dwell in this magnificent temple forever. He told the people that even though his father David wanted to build the temple, God ordained him, Solomon, to complete the task.

Standing before the altar, Solomon said a prayer to God. He praised God for keeping his promises and asked God to keep the promise he made to David to always have one of David's descendants upon the throne of Israel. In his prayer, Solomon recognized that God far exceeded anything human hands could make when he said, "But will God really dwell on earth? The heavens, even the highest heaven, cannot contain you. How much less this temple I have built!" (1 Kings 8:27). Solomon asked God to act justly and to have mercy when the people of Israel stood before the altar requesting forgiveness or to receive fair judgment. He asked God to adhere to the requests of foreigners and to support in Israel's military campaigns.

Following his prayer to the Lord, he faced the people again, blessed them and offered sacrifices before the Lord. The Lord sent fire from heaven to consume the offerings and the people worshiped and praised God. After the dedication, the people observed the festival of that time and then returned home with joyful hearts.

Soon thereafter, the Lord appeared to Solomon and told him that he heard his prayer and consecrated the temple. God promised Solomon that God's name, eyes, and heart would dwell there forever. He also promised Solomon that he would establish Solomon's royal throne over Israel forever. However, if anyone in Israel failed to observe God's commands or worshiped other gods, God would cut off Israel from the land and reject his temple. If Israel disobeyed, they would become an object of ridicule and the temple would become a heap of rubble.

SOLOMON'S PRAYER OF DEDICATION

"But will God really dwell on earth? The heavens, even the highest heaven, cannot contain you. How much less this temple I have built! Yet give attention to your servant's prayer and his plea for mercy, LORD my God. Hear the cry and the prayer that your servant is praying in your presence this day. May your eyes be open toward this temple night and day, this place of which you said, 'My Name shall be there,' so that you will hear the prayer your servant prays toward this place. Hear the supplication of your servant and of your people Israel when they pray toward this place. Hear from heaven, your dwelling place, and when you hear, forgive."
—1 Kings 8:27–30

HARMONIZING 1 KINGS 7:15-16 WITH 2 CHRONICLES 3:15

The two bronze pillars were 18 cubits (27 ft; 9 m) high and topped with decorative capitals. The decorative 5-cubit (7.5 ft; 2.29 m) capital "in the shape of lilies" is shown fitting down over the 17.5 cubit "pillar" described in 2 Chronicles 3:15. The hollow pillar, with a 9-inch (22.9 cm) weight-bearing surface at the top, creates a total pillar/capital unit of 18 cubits as recorded in 1 Kings 7:15.[4]

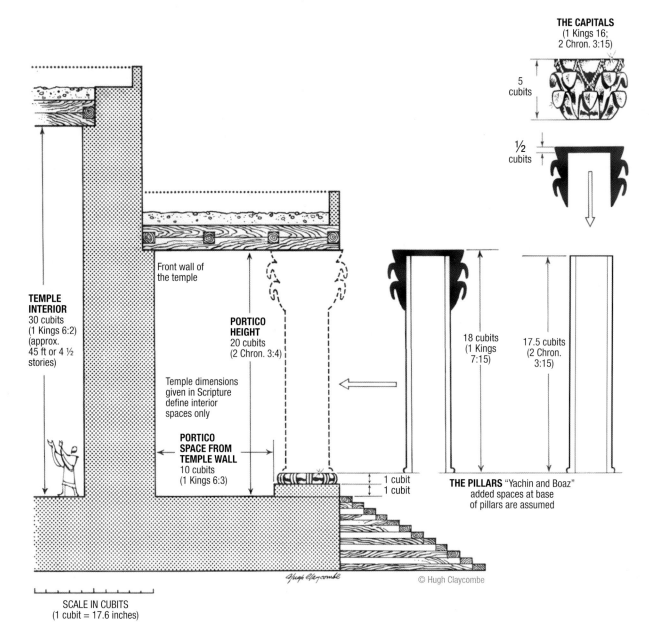

THE CAPITALS
(1 Kings 16;
2 Chron. 3:15)

5 cubits

½ cubits

Front wall of the temple

TEMPLE INTERIOR
30 cubits
(1 Kings 6:2)
(approx. 45 ft or 4 ½ stories)

PORTICO HEIGHT
20 cubits
(2 Chron. 3:4)

Temple dimensions given in Scripture define interior spaces only

PORTICO SPACE FROM TEMPLE WALL
10 cubits
(1 Kings 6:3)

18 cubits
(1 Kings 7:15)

17.5 cubits
(2 Chron. 3:15)

1 cubit
1 cubit

THE PILLARS "Yachin and Boaz"
added spaces at base of pillars are assumed

SCALE IN CUBITS
(1 cubit = 17.6 inches)

© Hugh Claycombe

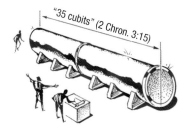

"35 cubits" (2 Chron. 3:15)

"In the front of the temple he [Solomon] made two pillars, which together were 35 cubits long" (2 Chronicles 3:15). This unusual way of expressing the 17.5 cubit length of each pillar may have occurred during the construction phase when the pillars were laying end to end.

THREE PARTS OF THE TEMPLE COMPLEX

The Courtyard

The temple complex consisted of three parts: the Courtyard, which was the outer area surrounding the temple, the Holy Place and Holy of Holies within the temple. The sacred items within the Courtyard enabled the priests to maintain proper ritual purity in order to gain access to the inner area (the temple itself).

THE OUTER DESIGN OF THE TEMPLE

The basic dimensions of the temple (based on the standard cubit of 18 inches) were 90 feet long (27.4 m) by 30 feet wide (9 m) by 45 feet high (14 m), totaling about 3,500 square feet (1,067 square meters)(1 Kings 6:2–3; 2 Chronicles 3:3–4). The temple would have fit inside a professional basketball court. A standard soccer field would be six times the size of Solomon's temple. The porch, at the front extending across the width of the temple, was 30 feet wide and 30 feet high (9 m x 9 m) (2 Chronicles 3:4). The temple had windows with decorated frames (1 Kings 6:4). The outer design included side chambers that consisted of three-storied rooms with a winding staircase that reached these rooms (1 Kings 6:5–8). The temple structure stood on a platform about 10 feet high (3 m). Ten steps, bordered on each side by cast bronze pillars, led upward to the entrance porch. The pillars were topped with molten bronze capitals each 7.5 feet (2.3 m) in height. Each capital was ornate, decorated with a lily network motif and twisted threads of chainwork into which were fastened 100 engraved pomegranates (1 Kings 7:17–20).

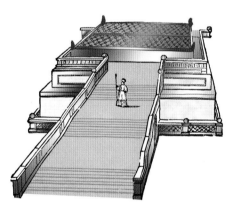

THE BRAZEN ALTAR

The brazen altar lay on the east side of the temple directly in front of the temple (2 Chronicles 4:1). The altar was made of fieldstones (Ex. 20:25) and measured 30 feet long by 30 feet wide (9 m x 9 m) and 15 feet high (4.6 m). The altar for the tabernacle was only 4.5 feet high (1.37 m) and didn't have steps, but since the altar at the temple was 15 feet high (4.6 m), it most likely had steps for the priests to climb in order to burn offerings and sacrifices. It is unclear exactly how much of this altar was polished bronze. But since the priests ministered barefoot in the temple complex, it is unlikely that the entire structure was covered in bronze, particularly the steps which the priests would have had to climb barefoot in the hot sun. There were also polished bronze pots, shovels, meat forks, and other articles necessary for making sacrifices and offerings upon the altar.

THE MOLTEN SEA (BRAZEN SEA/LAVER)

Near the altar, on the southeast corner of the temple, stood an immense cast metal water-basin or laver called the "brazen sea" or the "molten sea." This reservoir, 45 feet in circumference (14 m), 7.5 feet high (2.3 m), 3 inches thick (7.6 cm), and 15 feet (4.6 m) from brim to brim, held 11,000 gallons (41,640 liters) of water. It rested on the backs of 12 bronze oxen three facing north, three facing west, three facing south and three facing east (2 Chronicles 4:2–4). Two rows of 300 gourds encircled the sea below the rim. The purpose of the laver was to provide a source of water for the ritual cleansing of the priests who would officiate and the cleansing of vessels used in the sacrificial system.

TEN BRONZE BASINS

Near the molten sea were 10 bronze basins sitting in 10 bronze stands. Each stand was 6 feet long (18 m), 6 feet wide (18 m), and 4.5 feet high (1.4 m). Each basin was 18 feet (5.5 m) in circumference and held 240 gallons (908 liters) of water. The basins and stands were ornamented with figures of lions, oxen, and cherubim and decorated with wreaths of hanging work. The basins were stationed five on the north and five on the south sides of the Courtyard. The basins were used to transport water to various places around the temple, and much smaller sprinkling bowls were used to administer the water for ritual purification and cleansing of the priests.

The Holy Place

The largest room in the temple was called the Holy Place. Its walls were covered with cedar panels with elaborately carved cherubim overlaid with fine gold and decorated with palm trees and chains (2 Chronicles 3:5, 7). The floors were covered with boards of pine so that no stonework remained visible. This room was adorned with beautiful precious stones and its beams, thresholds, and doors were overlaid with gold (2 Chronicles 3:7–8). Objects inside this room included the lampstands, table(s) of the bread of the presence, the altar of incense as well as numerous tools and instruments used in priestly service.

THE GOLDEN LAMPSTAND (MENORAH)

Transferred from the tabernacle was the golden lampstand which had been beaten from a single piece of gold (Exodus 25:31–40). It is unclear exactly where the tabernacle menorah was placed in Solomon's temple, but it may have been hidden and stored in one of the temple chambers. Solomon had 10 new golden lampstands made and positioned them five on the north side and five on the south side of the Holy Place (2 Chronicles 4:7). There were also golden wick trimmers, tongs, and basins used in the priestly service.

THE TABLE(S) OF THE BREAD OF THE PRESENCE

The table of the bread of the presence held the 12 loaves of bread (showbread) made from fine flour (1 Kings 7:48). It was called the "bread of presence" because it was to be always before the Lord in his presence (Exodus 25:30). While there was one table in the tabernacle, Scripture indicates that there was as many as 10 tables for the bread of the presence at different times in the first temple period (1 Chronicles 28:16; 2 Chronicles 4:8). There were also 100 golden sprinkling bowls and pure gold dishes to be used in the priestly service (2 Chronicles 4).

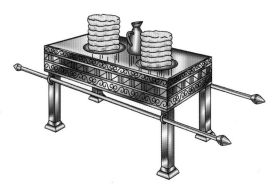

THE ALTAR OF INCENSE

The altar of incense was used to offer a special kind of incense to the Lord (Exodus 30:1–34; 1 Chronicles 28:18). The altar was cedar overlaid with pure gold. As with the altar in the tabernacle, on the Day of Atonement (Yom Kippur) the high priest took incense from this altar and brought it into the Holy of Holies. To accompany the altar were pure gold censers used in the priestly service.

The Holy of Holies (Most Holy Place)

The innermost room was separated from the Holy Place by a double veil of fabric and by a wall whose only door was kept closed, except on rare occasions. Access to this room, called the Holy of Holies, was forbidden to all except the high priest, and to him only once a year on the Day of Atonement. This room was constructed as a perfect cube about 30 feet (9 m) square and was gilded throughout with more than a ton of gold (2 Chron. 3:8). In the middle of this windowless room stood a raised platform, the covered top of Mt. Moriah that protruded within the Holy of Holies. Jewish tradition called it the "Foundation Stone" and believed it to be the center of the world and the point from which God created Adam. On this platform sat the most important of the holy furnishings—the ark of the covenant.

THE VEIL

The veil of the temple is mentioned only in 2 Chronicles 3:14: "He made the curtain of blue, purple and crimson yarn and fine linen, with cherubim worked into it." This design followed that of the tabernacle before it (Exodus 26:31–33; Hebrews 9:3) and was also followed in the second temple that came after it (Matthew 27:51). First Kings 8:8 says that the poles of the ark of the covenant were so long that they could be seen from the Holy Place. This means the poles protruded into the Holy Place and only a veil would have allowed this.

THE ARK OF THE COVENANT

Made out of acacia wood and overlaid with pure gold, the ark was the central focus of the temple. When Solomon brought the ark into the temple, there was "nothing in the ark except the two stone tablets that Moses had placed in it at Horeb, where the LORD made a covenant with the Israelites" (1 Kings 8:9). On the Day of Atonement, the high priest would sacrifice and sprinkle blood on the mercy seat—the top of the ark of the covenant where the winged cherubim faced each other—to atone for the sins of the people. The ark possibly rested within an incised base to prevent it from being unsteadied when the high priest used its long carrying poles to guide himself to the mercy seat. Solomon also made two 15-foot-high (4.6 m) olive wood cherubim overlaid with gold to overshadow the ark (1 Kings 6:23–28; 8:6–7).

THE MYSTERY OF THE LOST ARK

The ark of the covenant has always been shrouded in mystery. From the beginning, it was hidden from public view and approachable by only a select few. Once it was placed within the Holy of Holies, a specially constructed curtain was hung to prevent direct access to the ark. The Bible says that the ark was made of "acacia wood" (Exodus 25:10; KJV "shittim"). Acacia wood was considered so durable that the Septuagint (the Greek version of the Old Testament) translated the Hebrew "acacia wood" as "incorruptible wood." Magnifying this imperishable quality was the pure gold which overlaid the wood (Exodus 25:11). The ark disappeared with the destruction of the first temple in 586 BC. Therefore, in the second temple during the Day of Atonement the high priest could only pour the blood on the barren stone within the Holy of Holies where the ark would have been. Jewish tradition held that the ark was deposited before the first temple's destruction in a secret chamber beneath the Holy of Holies. Today in the news from time to time people will claim to know the whereabouts of the ark, but no conclusive proof has ever been offered.

Solomon's Temple Cutaway

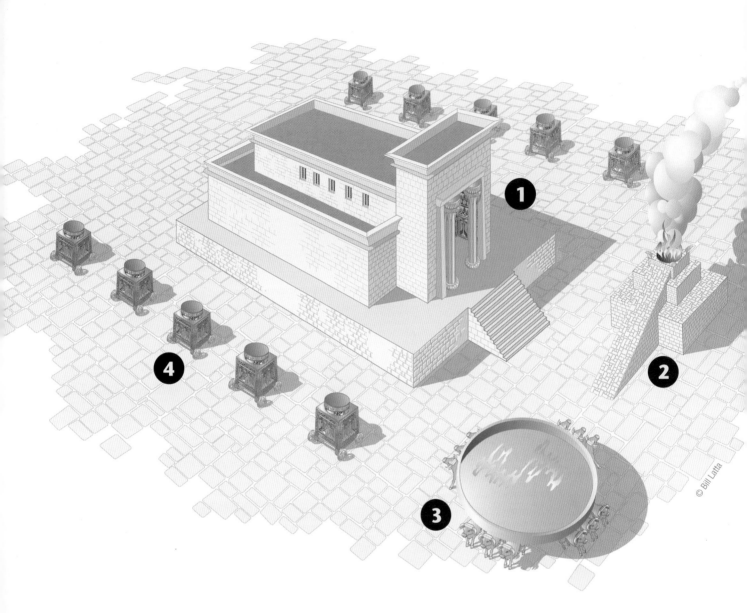

The Courtyard

1 The Temple

2 The Brazen Altar

3 The Molten Sea (Brazen Sea/Laver)

4 Ten Bronze Basins

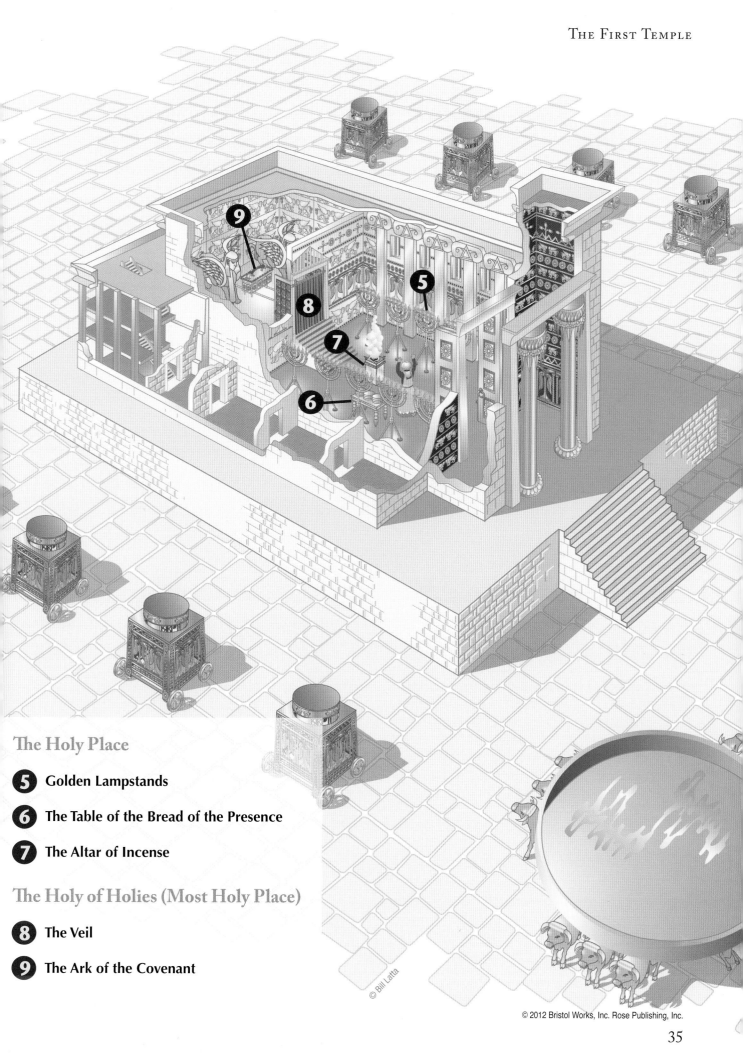

The Holy Place

5 Golden Lampstands

6 The Table of the Bread of the Presence

7 The Altar of Incense

The Holy of Holies (Most Holy Place)

8 The Veil

9 The Ark of the Covenant

© Bill Latta

Solomon's Temple Side View

1 **BRAZEN ALTAR.** Sacrifices took place upon this altar.

2 **ANIMALS FOR SACRIFICE.** Their blood would bear away the sin of a repenting and praying people. The animal was killed and its blood (life) drained away into vessels; the blood was placed on the horns and base of the altar. Other portions of the animal were eaten or burned.

3 **MOLTEN SEA (LAVER).** Held water used for ceremonial washing (1 Kings 7:23).

4 **BRONZE PILLARS.** "Yachin" and "Boaz" supported the roof of the Porch.

5 **HOLY PLACE**

6 **LAMPSTANDS AND TABLES.** The tables held the bread of the presence.

BEDROCK. The bedrock upon which the temple rested was once a threshing floor honorably purchased by Solomon's father, David (2 Samuel 24:24).

ART FORMS. Solomon carved cherubim and palm trees on the walls and "overlaid the whole interior with gold" (1 Kings 6). These were not objects of worship but only for God. Cherubim were winged spiritual beings guarding sacred objects. Scripture says the temple was decorated with various colors, turquoise, and marble, inlaid and painted possibly similar to other ancient temples.

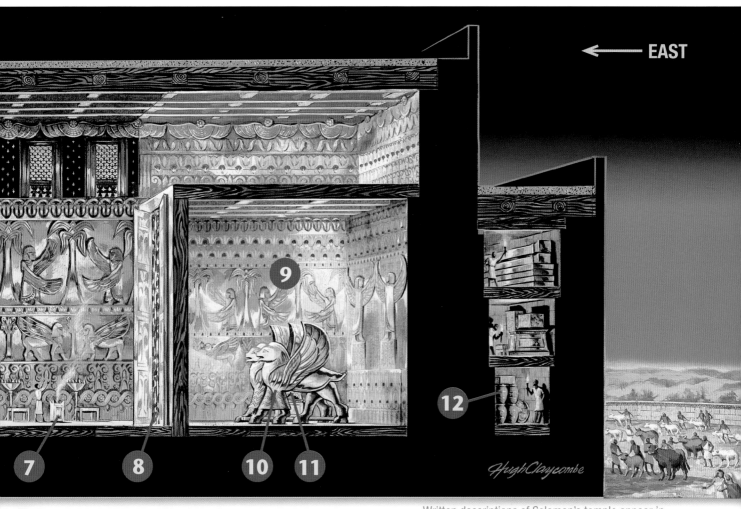

EAST

Written descriptions of Solomon's temple appear in Scripture but must be interpreted by each artist. No two illustrations look exactly alike. ©Hugh Claycombe

7 **ALTAR OF INCENSE.** Used for times of prayer.

8 **VEIL OR CURTAIN.** Made of blue, purple, crimson linen.

9 **HOLY OF HOLIES**

10 **CHERUBIM.** Massive sculptures touched each other wingtip to wingtip and wall to wall.

11 **ARK OF THE COVENANT.** Beneath the wings of guarding cherubim was this gold-covered chest carried from the wilderness of Sinai. Its lid was the place the high priest placed life (blood), and from this "mercy seat" God poured forth his mercy.

12 **STORE ROOMS (TREASURIES).** Three stories high, these rooms surrounded the temple on sides and rear, and contained the king's wealth.

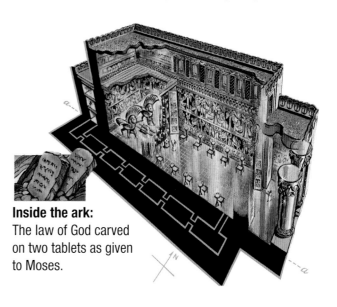

Inside the ark:
The law of God carved on two tablets as given to Moses.

The Temple in the Life of God's People

Eight Purposes of the Temple

When King David charged the people of Israel about the preparations for the first temple, he declared, "the work is great; for the temple is not for man, but for the Lord God" (1 Chronicles 29:1 NASB). In keeping with David's charge, the temple served eight basic purposes.

> "For the LORD has chosen Zion, he has desired it for his dwelling, saying, 'This is my resting place for ever and ever; here I will sit enthroned, for I have desired it.'"—Psalm 132:13–14

1. Station of the Divine Presence

After the Israelites had been brought safely through the Red Sea, Moses declared, "You will bring them in and plant them on the mountain of your inheritance—the place, LORD, you made for your dwelling, the sanctuary, Lord, your hands established" (Exodus 15:17). Even though God's glory temporarily appeared at the tabernacle, Moses' words pointed to the permanent manifestation of the Lord among his people in the temple in Jerusalem. In this way, while the transcendent God did not physically dwell in the temple, it was nevertheless a place where God's presence was accessible to humankind (1 Kings 8:27).

2. Sign of the Covenant

The presence of God in the temple was a witness to his covenant relationship with Israel:

- The construction of the temple on "the mount of the Lord" in Jerusalem (the land of Moriah) confirmed God's covenant with Abraham (Genesis 22:14) and his covenant with David (1 Kings 8:23–26; 2 Chronicles 3:1).

- The temple housed the ark of the covenant which contained the engraved stone tablets received by Moses on Mt. Sinai (1 Kings 8:3–9). The covenant with Moses promised God's protection and blessing to Israel if the people obeyed the terms of the covenant, but warned of God's judgment if the nation acted in disobedience (Leviticus 26).

3. Signal of the End of Exile

God told the children of Israel while in the wilderness that their experience of exile would end and rest begin only after they had settled in the Promised Land and established a central sanctuary (Deut. 12:9–14). This relationship to the temple was confirmed in Solomon's dedication prayer in which he praised God for giving rest to his people as he had promised to Moses (1 Kings 8:56).

THE SHEKINAH

In the Exodus wilderness experience, God's presence was represented with the cloud during the day and the column of fire during the night. God's glory—seen as a cloud—descended on the tabernacle (Exodus 40:34) and the temple (1 Kings 8:10) indwelling the buildings and demonstrating his presence.

The Jewish sages came to call this manifestation the *shekinah* from the Hebrew word *shakan*, meaning "to dwell." Biblical writers also expressed this concept of God's presence by saying that God caused his "name" to dwell there.

(See also 1 Kings 8:29; Jeremiah 7:12; Deuteronomy 12:11; 2 Chronicles 7:16; Ezra 6:12; Nehemiah 1:9.)

4. Socio-Political Institution

The temple served a significant role in the social and political life of the people by defining the patterns of:

- Legal matters
- Jewish daily life
- The cycle of festivals
- The annual pilgrimages
- The sacrificial rites
- The reading and study of the Torah

It also stood as a place of refuge for people accused of crimes such as treason (1 Kings 1:50–51; 2:28).

5. Symbol of National Sovereignty

The construction of the temple was a demonstration of national independence. It served as a national rallying point in times of repentance and disaster, such as a famine (1 Kings 8:33–38). When Israel was under the power of foreign nations, these nations punished political disloyalty through the destruction of the temple. Likewise, when the Jews returned from exile the rebuilding of the temple confirmed the return of a functioning state.

6. Secured National Blessings

At the time of the dedication of the temple, King Solomon declared the temple to be the place of national blessing (2 Chronicles 7:14). Since God was the source of all blessing and his presence was in the temple, it became the means of securing the covenantal promises (blessings).

7. Source of Worldwide Blessing

Solomon's prayer also indicated that the temple was to be a source of universal blessing. If foreigners came specifically to pray to the God of Israel at the temple, the Lord would hear their prayers (1 Kings 8:41–43).

8. Service as the Focal Point of Prayer

Because God's *shekinah* dwelt at the temple, those who prayed in the direction of the temple (that is, to God) would have his promise of protection (1 Kings 8:33, 42–43, 48–49). Focusing prayer on the temple recognized that God was the God of Israel and that he maintained his covenant with them. He was not to be found in any other place or in any other nation, for only the God at the temple in Jerusalem was the true God (Psalm 132:13–14; Zechariah 2:8; 8:2–3).

Priestly Duties

The daily duties laid out by the Lord for the priests in the temple were almost identical to the duties performed in the tabernacle. The priests served as the individuals who were the go-betweens of the people of Israel. They represented the people to God and God to the people, and they guarded the temple. Their basic duties within the temple were to make sacrifices and offerings, and maintain the presence of the Lord.

- Priests were responsible for blessing the people who brought the sacrifices and offerings. The priests would approve the sacrifices and offerings and burn them upon the brazen altar.

- Priests would then ritualistically purify themselves by bathing their hands and feet in the molten sea (laver) before entering the Holy Place.

- Inside the Holy Place, the priests were responsible for maintaining the bread of the presence on the tables. The priests would eat the bread weekly and replace it with fresh bread on the Sabbath, the seventh day of the week (1 Chronicles 9:32).

- The priests were also responsible for trimming the lamp wicks and making sure the oil did not burn out.

- The priests regularly made offerings of incense before the Lord on the golden altar.

A priest keeping the wicks of the lampstand burning. (Painting by Jerry Allison)

PRIESTS AND LEVITES: WHAT'S THE DIFFERENCE?

All priests are Levites, but not all Levites are priests. While priests (Hebrew *kohanim*) and Levites (Hebrew *levi'yim*) both belong to the same tribe of Levi, they come from different descendants within the tribe. Priests were male descendants of Aaron, Moses' brother, the first high priest. Levites (who served the temple) were any male descendants of the tribe of Levi, including the descendants of Moses and Miriam his sister. Priests and Levites shared the responsibility of serving in the tabernacle, and later, the temple. However, priests alone were responsible for conducting the sacrifices while the Levites assisted them in various duties such as construction and the maintenance of the temple.

The priests were divided into 24 groups with each member responsible for maintaining the schedule of offerings at the temple (1 Chronicles 24:3–5). Each of the 24 divisions consisted of six priestly families, with each of the six serving one day of the week except on the Sabbath when all six worked one after the other. The high priest was selected from among the priests and would serve for a generation.

The Levites were divided into three groups (Numbers 26:57): the descendants of Gershon (Gershonites), the descendants of Merari (Merarites), and the descendants of Kohath (Kohathites). The Levites functioned as the Levitical choir which played musical instruments and sang psalms during temple services. They also ministered to the priests, handled and stored the temple vessels, served as temple guards, functioned as teachers by translating and explaining the biblical text, and served as judges which included overseeing more than six cities of refuge (Numbers 18:2–6; 35:6).

THE HIGH PRIEST

The high priest was the ultimate mediator between God and the nation of Israel (Hebrews 5:1). The high priest needed to be a direct descendant of Aaron, Moses' brother. The current high priest would anoint one of his sons to succeed him as high priest.

The main duties of the high priest included:

- Sacrifices on the Day of Atonement
- Prayers of intercession before the mercy seat of the ark of the covenant on the Day of Atonement
- Management and supervision of the other priests

The high priest wore the following garments:

- **White linen tunic** (woven, one piece, close fitting).
- **Dark blue woven robe** (reached to knees and had blue, purple, and scarlet pomegranates upon the hem with bells of gold between each pomegranate).
- **Ephod** of gold, blue, purple, and scarlet entwined in linen (apron-like, shoulder piece coupled together by two edges).
- **Onyx stones** enclosed in pouches of gold with names of the 12 tribes engraved on them (six on each). One on each shoulder of the ephod.
- **Girdle** of the ephod (bound around waist).
- **Breastplate** of gold blue, purple, scarlet, and fine-twined linen doubled, four-square (about 8–10 in.; 20–26 cm):
  - Contained four rows of three stones (jewels). Each jewel contained the name of one of the 12 tribes set in gold.
  - Two rings of gold were in the top ends of the breastplate and two chains fastened to these rings, extending up to where they fastened at the shoulder pieces.
  - Two rings of gold were at the bottom ends and two rings in the ephod above the girdle at the waist laced together with blue lacing; the breastplate contained the Urim and Thummim.
- **The Miter or Turban** (crown of gold inscribed with "Holy to the Lord").

© 2012 Bristol Works, Inc. Rose Publishing, Inc.

SACRIFICES

The sacrificial system was the means by which atonement was made for people's sins. In obeying God's command to offer sacrifices, the people demonstrated their submission to God, their need for forgiveness, and their trust that he would provide the means of atonement. But why was there a need for *blood* sacrifices? Leviticus 17:11 explains: "For the life of a creature is in the blood, and I have given it to you to make atonement for yourselves on the altar." Human sin separates people from a holy God, and the cost of sin is the ultimate price. The apostle Paul in the New Testament echoes this truth: "For the wages of sin is death" (Romans 6:23). The sacrificial system was God's merciful provision for Israel so that the people could dwell with a holy God.

However, this sacrificial system for Israel was not a permanent institution in God's plan for humanity. God provided a perfect and ultimate sacrifice in his Son, Jesus Christ. Jesus' death on the cross was a voluntary sacrifice to atone for sin. Like the ancient Israelites who trusted in God's provision for animal sacrifices to atone for their sin, so too all those who trust in God's provision of his Son as the perfect sacrifice receive forgiveness of their sins. As the apostle Paul wrote, "For God was pleased to have all his fullness dwell in him [Jesus], and through him to reconcile to himself all things, whether things on earth or things in heaven, by making peace through his blood, shed on the cross" (Colossians 1:19–20).

Presenting Offerings at the Temple of Solomon. First temple priests prepare for the daily burnt-offering on the brazen altar. The Court of the Priest was in fact a slaughterhouse where animals were tethered to poles and ritually butchered on large blocks or tables.

(Artist: Balage Balogh, Archaeology Illustrated.com)

SACRIFICE	SIGNIFICANCE

Sin Offering and Guilt Offering
Leviticus 4–6; Numbers 15:1–12
 	
Sin offerings and guilt offerings focused on paying for sin. The sin offerings atoned for sins against God. The guilt offerings addressed sins against others, and included paying damages with interest. Various animals were offered, depending on the person's position and income. Priests and leaders, as examples to others, had to offer larger sacrifices for sin, while the poor offered what they could afford. Blood was sprinkled on the altar, the parts of the animals were burned, often with wine poured on them (drink offering). Other parts were roasted for the priests. Since the priests were full-time temple workers, sacrificed animals were their main source of food.
	Christ's Offering:
	    Isaiah 53:10; Matthew 20:28;
	    2 Corinthians 5:21
	
	Paying for Damages:
	    Matthew 5:23–24; Luke 19:1–10
	
	Poor: Luke 2:2–24; 21:1–4
	
	Leaders as Examples:
	    1 Timothy 3:1–7; 5:19–20
	
	Providing for Christian Workers:
	    Philippians 4:18; 1 Cor. 9:13–14;
	    1 Timothy 5:17–18

Burnt Offering
Leviticus 1
 	
This sacrifice represented complete dedication and surrender to God. The animal, usually an unblemished male, bore the worshiper's sins, and died in his/her place. After the blood was sprinkled on the altar, the animal was completely burned up. None of it was roasted for eating.
	Surrender:
	    Psalm 51:16, 17; Matthew 26:39;
	    Romans 12:1
	
	Dedication:
	    Philippians 2:17;
	    2 Timothy 4:6–7

Grain (Meal) Offering
Leviticus 2
 	
This offering was given to God in thankfulness. The people brought fine flour, unleavened cakes, or roasted grain to the priests. The priests burned a symbolic handful at the altar, and could partake of the rest. There was very little ceremony involved.
	Giving: Matthew 26:6-10;
	    2 Corinthians 9:7–11
	
	Praise:
	    Psalm 100; Hebrews 13:15–16
	
	Thankfulness:
	    Psalm 147; Philippians 4:6

Fellowship (Peace) Offering
Leviticus 2; 7:11–21
 	
This offering symbolized fellowship and peace with God through shed blood. After some meat was ceremonially waved and given to the priests, worshipers and their guests could share in the feast as a meal with God.
	God's Peace: Colossians 1:20;
	    Acts 10:36; Ephesians 2:14
	
	God's Feast: Luke 14:15–24;
	    1 Corinthians 11:17–26;
	    Jude 1:12; Revelation 3:20

The Feasts of Israel

The seven annual feasts of Israel served as sacred time that God set apart for his people to worship him in celebration and sacrifice. The feasts were times to:

- Remember what God had done in the past, such as his protection in the wilderness and his faithfulness to his promise to bring his people out of Egypt.

- Present grain offerings to thank God for his provision of the harvest.

- Conduct animal sacrifices for the atonement of the sins of the people.

- Have a day of rest unto the Lord when "no regular work" would be done.

These festivals originated in the wilderness during the time of the tabernacle. After God brought his people out of slavery in Egypt he revealed to Moses the seven annual holidays that he appointed as times to meet with him: "Speak to the Israelites and say to them: These are my appointed feasts, the appointed feasts of the Lord, which you are to proclaim as sacred assemblies" (Leviticus 23:1–2). When the first temple was built, the festival sacrifices that had taken place at the tabernacle were then done at the temple in Jerusalem. In this way the temple and Jerusalem became the central location for the celebrations.

Three of the seven biblical holidays were pilgrimage feasts when all Jewish males in the land were required to travel to Jerusalem to "appear before the Lord" (Deuteronomy 16:16). These were the Feast of Unleavened Bread (or Passover), the Feast of Weeks, and the Feast of Tabernacles. Appearing "before the Lord" at his temple was of utmost importance for Israel, and all males who were physically able to make the journey were obligated to attend.

Other Jewish festivals, such as the Feast of Lots (Purim as recorded in the Book of Esther) and the Feast of Dedication (Hanukkah) developed after the time of the first temple. (See *Hanukkah* on page 64.)

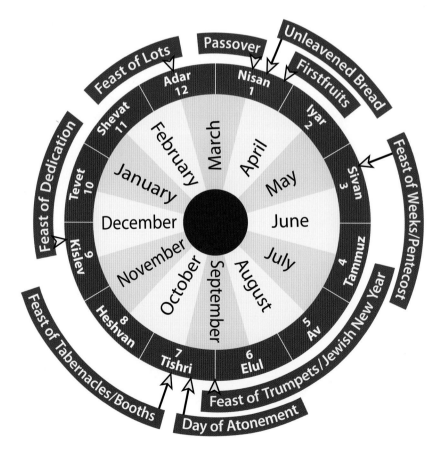

PASSOVER

Passover commemorated the Israelites' deliverance from slavery in Egypt. The tenth plague that the Lord sent to Egypt was the death of the firstborn males in every house. The only way to escape this judgment was if the doorframe of the house was covered with the blood of an unblemished lamb. The Lord "passed over" the homes with blood on the doorframes and spared the firstborns of that house. After that horrific plague, Pharaoh let the Israelites leave Egypt. The Passover celebration was to be a lasting ordinance for generations to come. It was observed in the first month of the biblical year (Exodus 12:2, 14).

New Testament: John the Baptizer declared Jesus as the "Lamb of God who takes away the sin of the world" (John 1:29, 35) and the apostle Paul calls Jesus "our Passover lamb" (1 Corinthians 5:7). Jesus was crucified in Jerusalem during Passover week, and the Last Supper is believed to have been a Passover meal. As the lamb in Old Testament times was a means of redemption of God's people, Jesus is the unblemished Lamb whose death on the cross provides redemption for all who believe in him.

FEAST OF UNLEAVENED BREAD

This feast was observed for seven days immediately following Passover. It is the first of the pilgrimage feasts. During this feast the Israelites ate unleavened bread. This bread, made in a hurry without yeast, represented how the Lord brought the Israelites out of Egypt in haste. In the Old Testament this feast is mentioned as a separate feast, however over the centuries the feasts of Passover, Unleavened Bread, and Firstfruits became incorporated into the week-long festival of Passover, and reference to Passover usually includes all three feasts.

New Testament: At age 12, Jesus traveled with his parents to Jerusalem to celebrate Passover (or Unleavened Bread). After the festival, his parents found him "in the temple courts, sitting among the teachers, listening to them and asking them questions" (Luke 2:41–50).

FEAST OF FIRSTFRUITS

Firstfruits was celebrated two days after Passover. On this day, the Israelites offered the first ripe sheaf (firstfruits) of barley to the Lord as an act of dedicating the harvest to him. On Passover, a marked sheaf of grain was bundled and left standing in the field. On the next day, the first day of Unleavened Bread, the sheaf was cut and prepared for the offering on the third day. On this third day (the day of Firstfruits), the priest waved the sheaf before the Lord. Firstfruits were the first and best grain of the harvest. In this way, the Israelites gave thanks to God by bringing him their very best.

New Testament: It was on this third day after Passover that Jesus rose from the dead. The apostle Paul calls Jesus "the firstfruits" among the dead (1 Corinthians 15:20–23). Paul also says in Romans 8:23: "Not only so, but we ourselves, who have the firstfruits of the Spirit, groan inwardly as we wait eagerly for our adoption to sonship, the redemption of our bodies." The Holy Spirit indwelling believers is their guarantee that, like Jesus, our earthly bodies will be redeemed and resurrected to eternal life.

FEAST OF WEEKS

Fifty days after Passover the Israelites celebrated the Feast of Weeks. This feast was also known as Shavuot, Pentecost, the Feast of Harvest, and the Latter Firstfruits because it was the time to present an offering of new grain of the summer wheat harvest to the Lord, showing joy and thankfulness for the Lord's blessing of the harvest. It is the second of the three pilgrimage feasts.

New Testament: It was on Pentecost that the disciples of Jesus were in Jerusalem in the upper room when the Holy Spirit descended upon them as tongues of fire (Acts 2).

FEAST OF TRUMPETS

This feast, the first of the three fall feasts, was observed on the first day of the seventh month of the biblical calendar. It was a day of rest commemorated with trumpet blasts and a food offering to the Lord. When the temple stood, silver trumpets were primarily used during this festival. However, after the temple was destroyed

in AD 70 along with most of the temple items including the silver trumpets, the shofar (ram's horn) trumpet became the most common trumpet used for this festival. Today, this holiday is celebrated as Rosh HaShanah, the Jewish New Year according to the civil calendar.

New Testament: The apostle Paul explains how a trumpet will one day sound the transformation of our earthly bodies: "Listen, I tell you a mystery: We will not all sleep, but we will all be changed—in a flash, in the twinkling of an eye, at the last trumpet. For the trumpet will sound, the dead will be raised imperishable, and we will be changed" (1 Corinthians 15:51–52).

DAY OF ATONEMENT

The Holy of Holies in the temple was entered only once a year on the Day of Atonement (Yom Kippur) when the high priest offered the blood sacrifice of atonement on behalf of the people. On this day the high priest sacrificed an animal to pay for his sins and the sins of the people. Carrying a censer of incense from the golden altar in the Holy Place, he entered the Holy of Holies and sprinkled blood on the mercy seat of the ark. When he was finished with the atonement sacrifice, a goat was released into the wilderness. This "scapegoat" symbolized the carrying away of Israel's sins (Leviticus 16:8–10, 20–22, 29–34).

New Testament: The author of the book of Hebrews calls Jesus our high priest saying, "When Christ came as high priest of the good things that are now already here ... he did not enter by means of the blood of goats and calves; but he entered the Most Holy Place once for all by his own blood, thus obtaining eternal redemption" (Hebrews 9:11–12).

FEAST OF TABERNACLES (BOOTHS)

This third pilgrimage feast was a week-long celebration of the fall harvest and a time to build booths (temporary shelters of branches) to remember how the people lived under God's care during their 40 years in the wilderness (Nehemiah 8:14–17). People covered their booths with citron, myrtle, palm, and willow (Leviticus 23:39–40).

New Testament: John 7 says that Jesus taught in the temple courts while pilgrims were gathered there for the Feast of Booths. By the time of Jesus, two additional ceremonies had become part of this celebration: the lighting of the great lights and the water-drawing ceremony. In the lighting ceremony, enormous lampstands were lit in the temple in the Court of the Women and people carrying torches marched around the temple. After this ceremony, but while the torches would still have been burning, Jesus declared, "I am the light of the world" (John 8:12). In the water-drawing ceremony, a priest would carry water from the Pool of Siloam to the temple as a prayer for rain for the harvest. The Gospel of John says, "On the last and greatest day of the festival, Jesus stood and said in a loud voice, 'Let anyone who is thirsty come to me and drink. Whoever believes in me, as Scripture has said, rivers of living water will flow from within them'" (John 7:37–38).

Sinai Wilderness

DESTRUCTION OF THE FIRST TEMPLE

God warned Solomon about the future destruction of the temple shortly after its completion. Solomon and his descendants had to remain loyal to God and keep God's commandments. If they didn't, God would cut off Israel from the land and he would destroy the temple. Even before his death, Solomon failed to remain loyal to God.

A preliminary judgment came shortly after Solomon's death when his son Rehoboam divided the kingdom. Jeroboam, who was not a descendent of King David, ruled the ten northern tribes (the "Northern Kingdom" or "Israel") and Rehoboam ruled the two southern tribes including the area of Jerusalem (the "Southern Kingdom" or "Judah").

	NORTHERN KINGDOM	SOUTHERN KINGDOM
Biblical Name	Israel	Judah (Includes Jerusalem)
Number of Tribes	10	2
Ruler after Solomon	Jeroboam, son of Nebat	Rehoboam, son of King Solomon, grandson of King David
Falls	722 BC, falls to Assyria	586 BC, falls to Babylon

During Rehoboam's reign, Pharaoh Shishak of Egypt attacked the Southern Kingdom targeting Jerusalem and the temple. The treasures of Solomon's palace, which housed 300 shields of beaten gold, were carried back to Egypt (1 Kings 14:25–26; 2 Chronicles 12:2, 9). Only because the royal court "humbled" itself at the instigation of God's prophet was the temple and Jerusalem spared further plunder (2 Chronicles 12:5–8).

However, in the Northern Kingdom, the Israelite king, Jeroboam, built alternate worship sites to keep the people from returning to the temple and coming back under the southern administration of Judah. Throughout the history of the Northern Kingdom, Israelite kings continued to set up pagan altars and "high places" (alternate worship sites) in the land. These actions brought about the exile of the Northern Kingdom under the Assyrians in 722 BC.

"I will remove Judah also from my sight, as I have removed Israel. And I will cast off Jerusalem, this city which I have chosen, and the temple of which I have said: 'My name shall be there.'"—2 Kings 23:27

The presence of the temple in Judah, and of reforming kings from King David's line like Josiah, delayed divine judgment on the Southern Kingdom for 135 years. During this period, many prophets, such as Isaiah and Jeremiah, warned the people of Judah that God would punish their disobedience by destroying the temple. In order to form treaties and alliances with other countries, Judah had to pay money to the more powerful nations. That money came largely from the temple treasury and the gold, silver, and precious materials adorning the temple. The people dismantled the temple piece by piece in order to make these payments. The prophets continued to warn Judah that God's judgment against their disobedience would eventually come.

The worst offense came with King Manasseh who committed acts of idolatry against the temple, even putting an idol in the Holy of Holies (2 Kings 21:4–8, 11–15). Judgment came under King Jehoiakim's reign in 605 BC, when Babylon's King Nebuchadnezzar invaded Jerusalem and carried away the king and thousands of his nobles and skilled laborers to Babylon (including Daniel and his friends).

A second invasion came in 597 BC and more people were deported. This invasion removed all of the remaining temple treasures to Babylon (2 Kings 24:13). The prophet Ezekiel may have been taken captive in this deportation (Ezekiel 9:1–8). Ezekiel saw a vision of the *shekinah* departing from the temple (Ezekiel 10:18–19). With the departure of God's presence, the temple was set apart for destruction. The prophets warned of this oncoming doom, and God's punishment for Judah's disobedience was about to reach its peak.

In 588 BC, King Nebuchadnezzar and the Babylonian army surrounded Jerusalem and kept the city under siege for 18 months leaving the city in famine. When the army breached the walls, the Judean army fled to the hills. One month later, Nebuzaradan, the commander of the Babylonian imperial guard, arrived at Jerusalem. He burned the temple, the palace, and all the buildings in Jerusalem. The two bronze pillars that had stood in front of the temple, the molten sea, and the ten bronze stands, were broken up and taken away (2 Kings 25:13; Jeremiah 52:17). The Babylonians destroyed the wall of the city and carried the people into exile.

Jerusalem Destroyed by Nebuchadnezzar. This painting depicts the destruction of the city of Jerusalem and the first temple in 586 BC. As the city burns in the background, captive Judeans are being herded toward Babylon where, according to God's judicial sentence, they remained for 70 years (Jeremiah 25:9–11). (Painting by William Brassey Hole)

TIME LINE: FIRST TEMPLE (960 BC–586 BC)

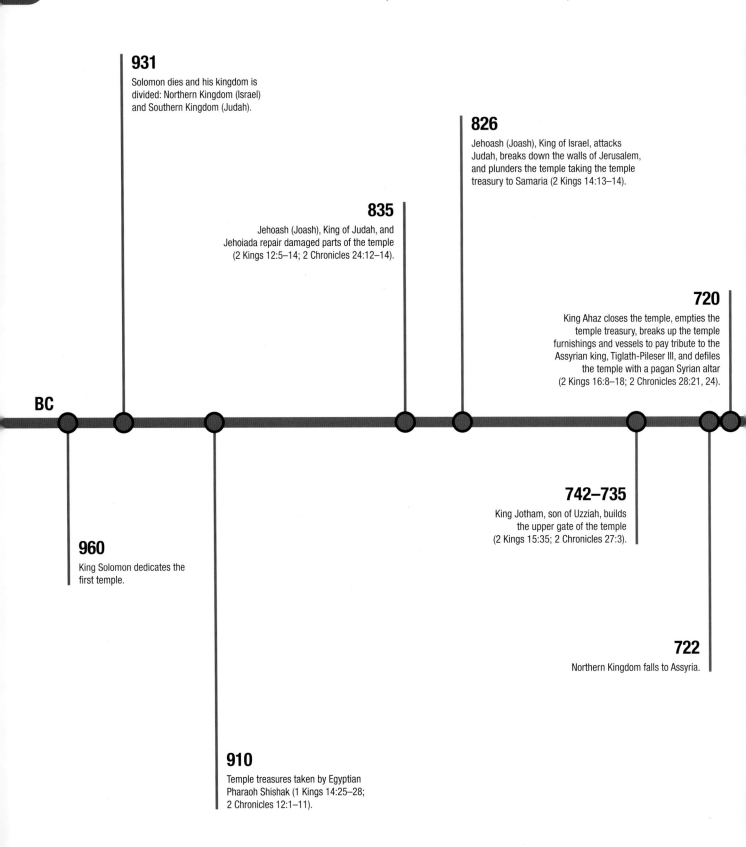

931
Solomon dies and his kingdom is divided: Northern Kingdom (Israel) and Southern Kingdom (Judah).

826
Jehoash (Joash), King of Israel, attacks Judah, breaks down the walls of Jerusalem, and plunders the temple taking the temple treasury to Samaria (2 Kings 14:13–14).

835
Jehoash (Joash), King of Judah, and Jehoiada repair damaged parts of the temple (2 Kings 12:5–14; 2 Chronicles 24:12–14).

720
King Ahaz closes the temple, empties the temple treasury, breaks up the temple furnishings and vessels to pay tribute to the Assyrian king, Tiglath-Pileser III, and defiles the temple with a pagan Syrian altar (2 Kings 16:8–18; 2 Chronicles 28:21, 24).

BC

960
King Solomon dedicates the first temple.

742–735
King Jotham, son of Uzziah, builds the upper gate of the temple (2 Kings 15:35; 2 Chronicles 27:3).

722
Northern Kingdom falls to Assyria.

910
Temple treasures taken by Egyptian Pharaoh Shishak (1 Kings 14:25–28; 2 Chronicles 12:1–11).

715

King Hezekiah opens the temple doors, cleanses the temple, returns temple vessels, restores ritual and Passover, and builds storehouses for temple contributions (2 Chronicles 29:3–19; 30:1–27; 31:11–12).

586

Nebuchadnezzar invades Jerusalem a third time and destroys the temple. Southern Kingdom of Judah falls to Babylon and Jews taken into captivity.

622

King Josiah of Judah, grandson of Manasseh, in restoring the temple, recovers one of the temple treasures, the *Torat Moshe* (autograph of the Pentateuch) that once was placed beside the ark and was apparently hidden in the temple during the time of Manasseh (2 Kings 22:8; 2 Chronicles 34:14–18). He commands the Levites to return the ark to the restored temple (2 Chronicles 35:3).

711

Hezekiah is forced to give up the temple treasuries and strip gold off the temple doors to pay tribute to the Assyrian king Sennacherib (2 Kings 18:15–16).

605

Babylon's King Nebuchadnezzar pillages the temple, taking articles and depositing them in the Babylonian temple at Shinar (2 Chronicles 36:7).

BC

695–642

King Manasseh of Judah places idols within the temple, including the Holy Place and the Holy of Holies. The ark and the other temple treasures were probably removed by the faithful Levites whom Manasseh deposed, to prevent their defilement. Manasseh later repents, but does not restore these treasures to the temple (2 Kings 21:4–7; 2 Chronicles 7–9, 15).

597

Nebuchadnezzar returns and further plunders the treasures of the temple (2 Kings 24:13; 2 Chronicles 36:7).

700

Hezekiah foolishly shows the treasures of the temple treasury and of the king's house to Berodach-baladan, a prince of Babylon and his envoys, an act the prophet Isaiah predicted would lead to the eventual plunder of the temple by the Babylonians (2 Kings 20:12–21; 2 Chronicles 32:31).

ARCHAEOLOGICAL DISCOVERIES

While the kingdoms of David and Solomon in the tenth century BC were once disputed, archaeological discoveries have affirmed the historicity of the biblical accounts.

1. CITY OF DAVID

Archaeology has uncovered the ancient "City of David" built upon and utilizing the remains of earlier Canaanite and Jebusite fortifications and water systems. Located in southern Jerusalem on a narrow ridge bordering the Kidron Valley, excavations have revealed a massive twelve-story high stepped-stone structure from the thirteenth century BC that is believed to be the place upon which David began to build his city (2 Samuel 5:9). This foundational structure may have served as a retaining wall buttressing King David's Fortress of Zion, as the recent discovery of monumental buildings just above have been interpreted as the remains of David's palace.

It was on the elevated extension of a ridge above this palace (the Ophel) that Mt. Moriah was situated and the first temple built by Solomon. In 2010 a city wall with a gatehouse dating to the late tenth century BC was discovered in the Ophel. A partial inscription in ancient Hebrew found on one of several large storage jars unearthed in the complex indicated it belonged to a high-level government official. Seal impressions discovered in the site also argue for a royal context. This fits well with the biblical record of royal construction that employed skilled Phoenician architects and engineers to construct the first temple (1 Kings 7:13–14), and may even specifically mention these structures: "...until he [Solomon] had completed building his own house, and the house of the Lord, and the wall around Jerusalem" (1 Kings 3:1).

According to some archaeologists, this wall probably connected with the City of David and fits with the biblical description that King Solomon built a fortification line around his new constructions of the temple and the king's palace.

Also, scores of clay *bullae* (small seals stamped with the sender's name and attached to documents) were discovered in a room in David's City that had been burned in the Babylonian destruction of

Stepped-stone structure which served as part of the foundation for the City of David. (Photo courtesy of Kim Walton)

the first temple. Many personal names mentioned in
Jeremiah and Chronicles were found including that
of "Azaryahu son of Hilkiyahu," who was a member
of the family of high priests who served at the end
of the first temple period (1 Chronicles 9:10).

2. TEL DAN INSCRIPTION

Two fragments of a monumental stele were
discovered at Tel Dan (Golan Heights) built by
Hazael, King of Damascus (or one of his sons)
in tribute of a victory over local enemies, which
included the Israelites. (A stele is stone or wooden
slab used for commemorating important people and
events.) The significance of the Aramaic inscription
is its mention of "the house of David." It provides
archaeological evidence for the existence of the
biblical King David and his royal dynasty.

3. KHIRBET QEIYAFA

At the site of Khirbet Qeiyafa, a provincial town
in Judea in the Elah Valley region, archaeologists
uncovered impressive fortifications that date from
the tenth century BC, the time of King David.
They also discovered an ostracon (inscription on
a potsherd) of a legal document from this same
period. Some archaeologists believe this inscription
to be the earliest known Hebrew writing. The
content of the inscription—which mentions social
obligations to widows, slaves, and the poor—reflects
elements found in the Old Testament.

"House of David" (Epigraphic Hebrew)

4. "SON OF IMMER" BULLA

Among the many finds of the Temple Mount Sifting Project is a clay bulla (a small seal
stamped with the sender's name and attached to documents) with an ancient Hebrew
inscription, "Belonging to Gaalyahu son of Immer." This man was probably
associated with the temple precincts and the priestly family of Immer mentioned
in Jeremiah 20:1.

"Son of Immer" bulla
(Zachi Zweig/Temple Mount Sifting Project)

Temples in the Ancient Near East

The description of the temple in the Bible was written in Ancient Hebrew, a language last used 500 years before Jesus. Language changes so much over time that some of the technical words for the ancient construction industry are difficult to translate.

However, scholars have noted that the temple in Jerusalem had similar features to other temples of its time and region. The basic temple design in Semitic religions was a courtyard surrounding a sacred space that was divided into two or three sections (called a tripartite). Many Phoenician (Sidonian) architects and craftsmen advised and designed the first temple's construction (1 Kings 7:13–14) patterning it after foreign temples. There was a divinely revealed plan for God's temple, but this accommodated the local culture and architecture. The construction of the second temple under Zerubbabel also involved Phoenician workmen (Ezra 3:7–10). Excavated Phoenician temples contain many similarities to the temple in Jerusalem. Such archaeological information concerning comparative temples makes it possible to reconstruct a reasonably accurate portrait of the temple built by Solomon.

The temple of 'Ain Dara in Syria is one of the best examples of the Solomon-style temple. Because no remains of Solomon's temple exist and the biblical descriptions contain many unclear architectural terms, the 'Ain Dara temple may offer the best means of reconstructing what the first temple may have looked like. The 'Ain Dara temple shares 33 of the 65 architectural elements with Solomon's temple. They both share the same three-division, long room plan. Solomon's temple was slightly wider than the 'Ain Dara temple, but much longer. Each was built on a platform stationed within a courtyard, and each had similar reliefs that decorated their walls. The elevated podium at the back of the 'Ain Dara temple, separated from the forepart by a screen, was almost identical to the Holy of Holies. The only major difference between Solomon's temple and 'Ain Dara is that 'Ain Dara had an antechamber.[5]

Ruins of the temple at 'Ain Dara in modern day Syria. (Photo courtesy of John Monson)

The 'Ain Dara temple may help resolve a long-standing debate over whether the huge pillars that flanked the entrance to Solomon's temple were load-bearing or free-standing. While only the basalt bases remain of the two massive columns (about 3 ft in diameter; 0.91 m) at the entryway of the 'Ain Dara temple's porch, these seem to have certainly supported a roof protecting the porch. This provides evidence that Solomon's pillars (Yachin and Boaz) were indeed load-bearing.

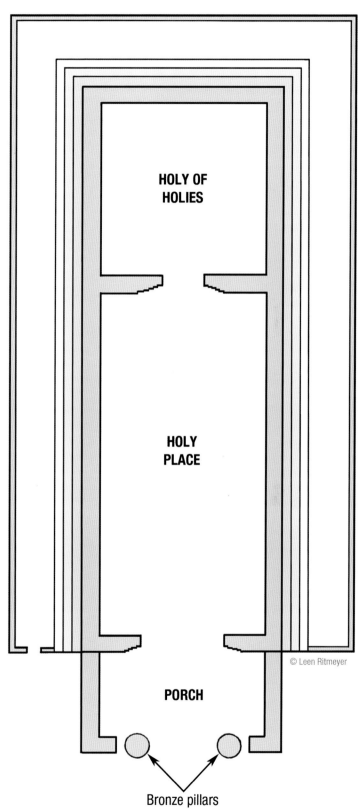

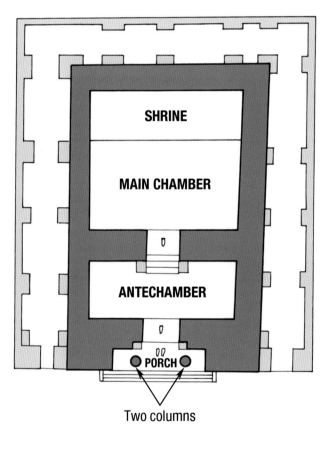

'Ain Dara Temple

Solomon's Temple

© Leen Ritmeyer

Messiah in the Temple Foundation

God's Permanent Sanctuary Rebuilt:
The Second Temple

Zerubbabel's Temple

Return from Exile

When the Babylonians burned Jerusalem and destroyed the temple, the people's worst nightmare came true. King Nebuchadnezzar's armies dragged the best and brightest into exile more than 700 miles (1,127 km) from home. But God's plan was greater. The Lord promised to look after his people as they lived in Babylon. According to the biblical prophets, God would restore the temple after a 70-year period of divine discipline (Jeremiah 25:10–12; Daniel 9:2–19).

The time of restoration was set in motion by the overthrow of Babylon by the Medes and the Persians (2 Chronicles 36:20–21; Daniel 5:30–31). The prophet Isaiah even revealed the name of the Persian monarch, Cyrus, who would return the exiles and provide for the rebuilding of the temple (Isaiah 44:28; Ezra 1:1–3). Josephus, the first-century Jewish historian, recorded the tradition that Cyrus the Great's actions were prompted by this prophecy of Isaiah. Josephus wrote, "…by reading the book which Isaiah left behind of his prophecies; for this prophet had spoken thus to him in a secret vision: 'My will is, that Cyrus … send back My people to their own land, and build My Temple.' Accordingly, when Cyrus read this, and admired the divine power, an earnest desire and ambition seized upon him to fulfill what was so written."[6]

Captivity of the Jews in Babylon
(Painting by William Brassey Hole)

In 538 BC, Cyrus issued an official edict allowing the Jews to return and rebuild the temple (2 Chron. 36:22–23). This edict was recorded on a clay cylinder and appears twice in the Bible in two languages: Ezra 1:1–4 in Hebrew and Ezra 6:1–5 in Aramaic. Once this word was given, Zerubbabel led about 50,000 Jews back to Jerusalem, carrying with them 5,400 of the temple vessels that had been taken to Babylon and stored in the Babylonian temple at Shinar (Ezra 1:7–11; 2:1–68; Daniel 1:2; 5:2; Isaiah 52:11–12; Jeremiah 27:18–22).

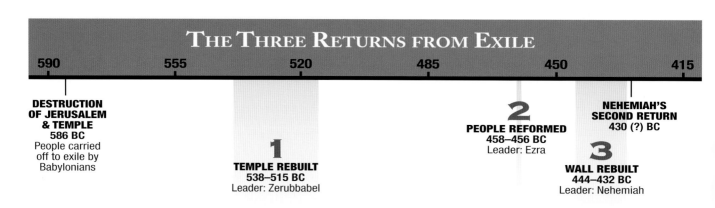

The Three Returns from Exile

590   555   520   485   450   415

DESTRUCTION OF JERUSALEM & TEMPLE
586 BC
People carried off to exile by Babylonians

1
TEMPLE REBUILT
538–515 BC
Leader: Zerubbabel

2
PEOPLE REFORMED
458–456 BC
Leader: Ezra

3
WALL REBUILT
444–432 BC
Leader: Nehemiah

NEHEMIAH'S SECOND RETURN
430 (?) BC

The Site and Construction

God designated the site of Mt. Moriah and the divine presence once dwelt there and promised to return to the same site (Exodus 15:17; 1 Kings 8:10–13; 1 Chronicles 21:18–28; Ezekiel 43:1–7). The location for rebuilding the temple was confirmed at its original site and on its original foundation.

Under the leadership of Zerubbabel and Joshua the high priest, the people laid the foundation for the first phase of the second temple (Haggai 2:2). Following the precedent set in preparation for the first temple, the people gave generously to the sacred treasury for this second temple (Ezra 2:68–69). The first act of restoration was building the altar of burnt offering, which allowed the people to reinstate the sacrificial system and observe the biblical festivals (Ezra 3:1–5). With the expertise of Phoenician workmen, the foundations for the second temple were laid in 535 BC (Ezra 3:7). It appears that the design of the second temple followed closely that of the first, but without an adjacent royal compound (Haggai 2:3). (The royal compound had included the palace and the administrative buildings of Solomon such as the House of the Forest of Lebanon.)

Cyrus Cylinder (sixth century BC). Written in Babylonian cuneiform, it describes King Cyrus's victory over Babylon and his permission of free worship. It reads, "I returned to sacred cities on the other side of the Tigris, the sanctuaries of which have been in ruins for a long time, the images which to live therein and established for… them permanent sanctuaries. I gathered all their inhabitants and returned them to their habitations."

Due to Samaritan resistance, construction was put on hold for 15 years. However, through the exhortation of the prophets Haggai and Zechariah, the work was resumed in 520 BC. Furthermore, a decree from Persia's King Darius I provided official sanction and support from local taxes to finance the completion of the structure (Ezra 6:1–15). This new temple was dedicated on March 12, 515 about 20 years after the return from exile, ending the 70-year desolation of Jerusalem.

Compared to the first temple, the second was regarded as inferior by those who had seen the first temple. It lacked a royal compound, the two entrance pillars, the two olive wood cherubim, and the most sacred furnishing—the ark of the covenant. The second temple also lacked the

Rebuilding of the walls of Jerusalem under Nehemiah. The workers, conscripted from among the 42,360 Jews that returned to Jerusalem under Zerubbabel to rebuild the second temple (Ezra 2), labored with construction tools in one hand and a weapon at the ready. This was because of the constant threat to the builders from neighboring enemies (Nehemiah 4:11–22). At the time Jerusalem's walls were being rebuilt, the construction of the second temple had already been completed (Ezra 3:1–13; 5:1–17; 6:1–18).

(Painting by William Brassey Hole)

shekinah glory that had signified the presence of God at the temple. For these reasons, the Bible notes that at the time this temple's foundations were laid many of the priests and Levites who were old enough to have seen the first temple wept (Ezra 3:12–13).

Who's Who in the Second Temple

NAME	DESCRIPTION
Zerubbabel	The first governor of Judah and descendant of David. In 538 BC, he led 42,360 Jews back from exile to Jerusalem and the Persian province of Judah. He was charged by King Cyrus the Great to supervise the rebuilding of the temple in Jerusalem.
Joshua the High Priest	The first high priest in the second temple. Joshua returned from exile with Zerubbabel and assisted in the rebuilding of the temple.
Haggai	A Hebrew prophet during the building of the second temple in Jerusalem. Haggai arrived on the scene 18 years after the Jews returned from exile. After experiencing resistance from local Samaritans, the rebuilding of the temple was put on hold. Through Haggai's efforts, the work on the temple was resumed.
Zechariah	A Hebrew prophet and contemporary with Haggai. He also urged the people to resume building the temple in 520 BC after a lapse in construction of 15 years. Additionally, a decree from Persia's King Darius I provided official sanction and support from local taxes to finance the completion of the structure (Ezra 6:1–15).
Ezra	A descendant of Aaron who was sent to Jerusalem by King Artaxerxes of Persia to teach the Law of Moses to the people in Judah. Once in Jerusalem, Ezra recognized several impurities in the land and strove to purify and cleanse the community.
Nehemiah	The cupbearer to King Artaxerxes of Persia who, after recognizing the desperate need to rebuild the walls of Jerusalem, asked his king if he could return to head up the task. Thirteen years after sending Ezra to Jerusalem, King Artaxerxes sent Nehemiah to Jerusalem as the governor of Judah with a mission to rebuild the walls. Once in Jerusalem, Nehemiah faced much opposition from Judah's enemies. Nehemiah also helped Ezra purify the community.

The Temple Mount

Josephus implies that Solomon's temple was built on a square Temple Mount and that over time the people increased the size of the Temple Mount.[7] Therefore, the later size of the Temple Mount was greater than that of Solomon's. At some point the Temple Mount became a 500-cubit square (861 ft, 262 m, or 17.2 acres, based on the Royal cubit of 20.67 in.).[8] Sources imply that the second temple builders also followed the lines of the 500-cubit-square Temple Mount.[9]

Through examining structures around and on the Temple Mount, archaeologists have discovered extensions added to the original Temple Mount. The evidence for locating the sides of the original Temple Mount are:

- The Western Wall: A now-covered wall preserved as the lowest step of the staircase at the northwest corner of the platform.

- The Northern Wall: Remains of a quarried rockscarp (a rock that protrudes like a cliff), found in the nineteenth century by Charles Warren, and whose lines form right angles with the step/wall and the Eastern Wall.

- The Eastern Wall: The unchanged line of the Eastern Wall between the sixth century BC offset in the north and the bend in the south equals 500 cubits.

- The Southern Wall: Measuring from the southeast corner (indicated by the bend) parallel to the northern wall to the intersection with continuation of the step/wall.

Nehemiah Petitions King Artaxerxes. "Then I prayed to the God of heaven, and I answered the king, 'If it pleases the king and if your servant has found favor in his sight, let him send me to the city in Judah where my ancestors are buried so that I can rebuild it'" (Nehemiah 2:4–5). (Painting by William Brassey Hole)

THE TEMPLE IN SAMARIA

According to the books of Ezra and Nehemiah, the northern dwellers of the land opposed the recently arrived Jews. Having come from Persia and Babylon, after decades of exile, the Jews desired to rebuild Jerusalem and, most importantly, rebuild the temple. However, they faced opposition from a group of people identified as "the people of the land." In later times, these people came to be identified as the Samaritans.

Because of strong disagreement with the Jews, the Samaritans built their own temple on Mt. Gerizim in Samaria which became their sanctuary. Archaeological excavations suggest that this temple was built in the fifth century BC. Many years later, the Samaritan temple was destroyed by the Maccabean leader John Hyrcanus around 129 BC. The discovery of the remains of the Samaritan temple have allowed archaeologists to confirm the design of the rebuilt temple in Jerusalem. The temple on Mt. Gerizim included gates, altars, and six-foot thick walls.

The New Testament account of Jesus talking with the Samaritan woman in John 4 shows how the Jews and Samaritans continued to disagree about the legitimate place of worship, Samaria or Jerusalem.

Expansion of the Temple Mount

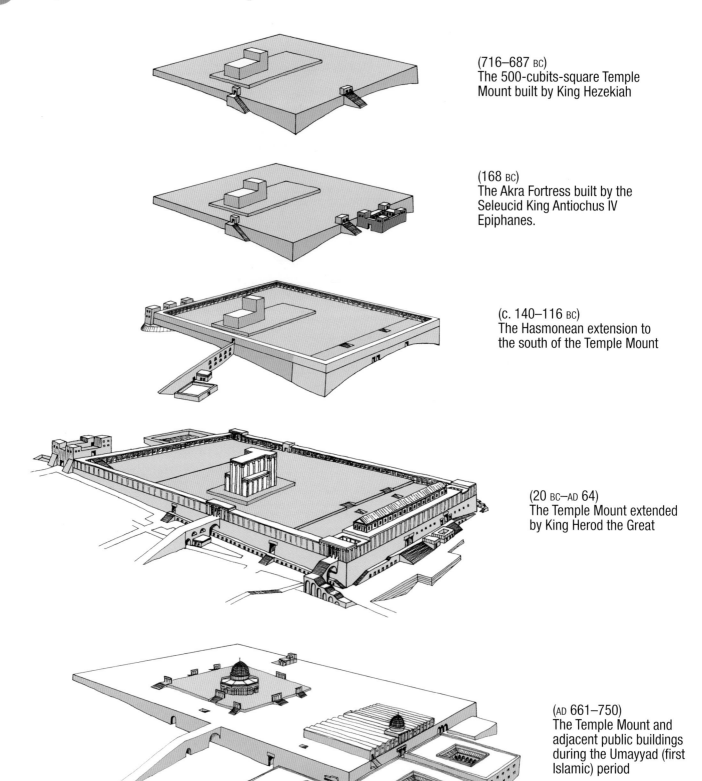

(716–687 BC)
The 500-cubits-square Temple Mount built by King Hezekiah

(168 BC)
The Akra Fortress built by the Seleucid King Antiochus IV Epiphanes.

(c. 140–116 BC)
The Hasmonean extension to the south of the Temple Mount

(20 BC–AD 64)
The Temple Mount extended by King Herod the Great

(AD 661–750)
The Temple Mount and adjacent public buildings during the Umayyad (first Islamic) period

© Leen Ritmeyer

Peace, Politics, and Pollution

The temple built by Zerubbabel stood for 350 years without suffering invasion or desecration from the surrounding nations. However, in the second century BC, Jerusalem came under the control of the Seleucids (an empire founded by Seleucid, one of Alexander the Great's generals). Early in this period, Simon, the son of the high priest Onias II, made extensive repairs to the temple.[10]

Initially the Seleucid ruler, Antiochus III, granted the inhabitants of Jerusalem the right to live according to their customs as long as they did not interfere with his foreign policy. However in 175 BC, under the reign of the Antiochus IV Epiphanes (175–164 BC), two Jewish factions—one conservative (strict Jewish culture) and the other Hellenist (pro-Greek culture)—contended for the high priesthood. As a promoter of the Greek culture, Antiochus sided with the Hellenistic party and for a sum of money appointed Jason as high priest in place of Onias III. Jason and his followers aimed to transform Jerusalem into a Greek city and incorporate Greek elements into Jewish practice. He went so far as to construct a gymnasium (which was a place that trained young men to become Greek citizens) near the temple itself.

As the bidding wars for the priesthood continued, Antiochus invaded Jerusalem in 170 BC, killed many Jews, and plundered the temple. At the southern end of the square Temple Mount, he constructed the Akra fortress, which was a tower from which he could secure control over the Temple Mount. On December 6, 167 BC, Antiochus polluted the sanctuary's altar by sacrificing unclean animals such as a pig and by placing in the temple an idolatrous statute of the Greek god Zeus Olympias that bore an image of Antiochus's own face. This was in keeping with the coinage he issued which showed Antiochus enthroned with the words, "King Antiochus, god manifest."

DANIEL'S PROPHECY

In the book of Daniel, chapters 10–12, the prophet Daniel who lived during the exile in Babylon (sixth century BC) receives a series of revelations regarding the fate of the Jewish people. Some Bible scholars interpret these visions as representing the history from Daniel's time to the destruction of the second temple, with the bulk of the prophecy concerning Antiochus IV Epiphanes. In Daniel 11:21, Antiochus is called a "contemptible person" who "will invade the kingdom when its people feel secure, and he will seize it through intrigue." The "prince of the covenant" who will be "broken" in Daniel 11:22 is understood to be Onias III the high priest who opposed Antiochus's Hellenization of the Jews and was stripped of his office. (See also Daniel 8:23–25.)

Antiochus IV Epiphanes coin which reads, "King Antiochus, god manifest."

The Jewish priest Judas Maccabeus led his family and followers in a successful revolt against the Seleucids that liberated Jerusalem. On the 25th of the Hebrew month of Chislev (that year it fell on December 4) 164 BC, the temple was purified and rededicated and the daily offerings (*tamid*) were restored. This celebration of dedication became a festival known as the

Feast of Dedication (Hanukkah). As a result, the independent rule of the Maccabean (or Hasmonean) dynasty was established over all Judea. These rulers made renovations to the deteriorating temple structure, and because of the growing threats they added constructions to the temple complex.

The Romans Conquer Jerusalem and Enter the Temple

Following the victory of the Maccabees over the Seleucids, the last of the Maccabean brothers, Simon, was declared to be high priest and leader of the nation. Thus the Hasmoneans (the family name of the Maccabees) became the established high priestly family, and they also assumed the kingship and other royal titles. Under the Hasmonean dynasty, Jewish conquests continued and they conquered both Samaria and Idumea (a region between the Dead Sea and the Gulf of Aqaba).

Power struggles within the dynasty and disputes about the Hasmoneans holding both priestly and kingly offices, led to skirmishes and eventually civil war. Two brothers, Hycranus II and Aristobulus II, vied for the position of high priest. Their feud paved the way for the Roman general Pompey to exploit the situation and gain control of Jerusalem. Both brothers appealed to Pompey to support their cause, but in 63 BC Pompey invaded the city and stormed the Temple Mount.[11]

When Pompey tried to enter the temple, thousands of Jews threw themselves to the ground before the general and begged him not to desecrate the Holy Place. Such a display convinced Pompey that the temple must contain great riches or some hidden secret, so he marched into the Holy Place, tore away the veil of separation and marched into the Holy of Holies. The Roman historian Tacitus (AD 56–117) described what happened next: "By right of conquest he [Pompey] entered their temple. It is a fact well known, that he found no image, no statue, no symbolical representation of the Deity: the whole presented a naked dome; the sanctuary was unadorned and simple."[12] According to tradition, when Pompey emerged from the temple he looked around at the Jews and declared, "It is empty; there is nothing there but darkness!" Pompey's confusion is an example of the misunderstanding the Gentile rulers had about the temple and its invisible God. However, when Pompey ordered his soldiers to tear down the walls of the city, he kept the temple intact.

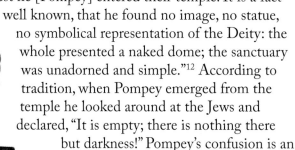

Roman General Pompey

HANUKKAH

Hanukkah, which means "dedication" or "consecration," is a festival that celebrates the rededication of the temple in Jerusalem in 164 BC. Hanukkah is a joyful celebration reminding people of God's faithfulness and gracious provision. It is also called the Feast of Dedication, and the Gospel of John records Jesus celebrating this festival in Solomon's Porch at the temple.

According to the traditional story of Hanukkah, after cleansing the temple, the pious Jews desired to rededicate the temple to the Lord. To do this, the lights in the temple, which symbolized the presence of God, had to be permanently alight. The priests only had enough lamp oil for one day, and the process to purify new oil would take eight days. So the priests prayed to God and set the lamps alight with the oil they had for one day. However, God performed a great miracle and the lamp flames burned for the eight additional days needed to purify new oil, so the flame never went out. For this reason, the Hanukkah candelabra used in the celebration has nine candles, one for each day the flame continued to burn.

TIME LINE: SECOND TEMPLE (585 BC–63 BC)

520–515
Zerubbabel, a descendant of David, rebuilds and dedicates the temple and restores the sacrificial system with assistance of the Persian king, Darius (Ezra 3:1–13; 5:1–17; 6:1–18).

573
The prophet Ezekiel, in Babylonian exile, has a vision of a magnificent temple (Ezekiel 40–48). Some Bible scholars believe this vision is of the future temple in the millennial (1,000-year) kingdom.

445
Nehemiah returns to Jerusalem from Persia to rebuild the walls of the city and protect the Temple Mount (Nehemiah 1–7:4).

168 BC–AD 73
The Jewish apocryphal, apocalyptic, and pseudepigraphical writings, including the Dead Sea Scrolls (such as the *Temple Scroll*[15]), are produced and include prophecies about the restoration of the temple.

164
On December 25, Judas Maccabeus restores Jewish ritual by cleansing and rededicating the temple (first Hanukkah) after a successful revolt against Seleucids.[16]

175
Antiochus IV Epiphanes, Seleucid king of Syria, pillages the temple. In 167, the soldiers of Antiochus defile temple; the king stops Jewish sacrifices and institutes the worship of Olympian Zeus in the temple.[14]

AC ———— BC

538
Cyrus issues a decree allowing Jews in exile to return to Jerusalem and rebuild the city and the temple, and returns temple vessels taken by Nebuchadnezzar (2 Chronicles 36:22–23; Ezra 1:1–11; 6:3–15).

The prophet Daniel prays concerning Jerusalem's and the temple's restoration and receives the prophecy of the 70 weeks concerning the Messiah's death in Jerusalem, the destruction of the temple, and its rebuilding and desecration (Daniel 9:1–27). Daniel also receives a vision of the defiling of the temple (Daniel 11:31). Some Bible scholars conclude that this vision is of the second temple (Zerubbabel's temple) defiled by Antiochus IV Epiphanes who placed a statue of the Greek god Zeus in the Holy Place.

332
Alexander the Great conquers Jerusalem and, according to Josephus, prostrates himself before the high priest and offers a sacrifice in the temple.[13] This is probably an embellished account given to explain why Alexander spared the temple.

67
Aristobulus besieges Jerusalem and substitutes a pig for a sheep in an attempt to end the temple sacrifices (which were stopped on the seventeenth of *Tammuz*). The result of this family war between Aristobulus and his brother Hycranus led to the intervention of Rome and the end of Jewish independence.

63
Roman emperor Pompey conquers Jerusalem and enters the Holy of Holies.

539
On October 11–12, Babylonian king Belshazzar desecrates temple vessels at a pagan feast (Daniel 5:1–4) and Persian monarch Cyrus the Great conquers Babylon.

HEROD'S TEMPLE

Herod's Plan for a Bigger, Better Temple

The Romans appointed over Judea a man named Antipater the Idumean or Edomite. (Idumeans were a non-Jewish Semitic group from the region between the Dead Sea and the Gulf of Aqaba.) Following Antipater's death, the Romans commissioned his son Herod to end further resistance from the Hasmonean rulers.

In 37 or 36 BC, Herod laid siege to Jerusalem and captured the Temple Mount, destroying a portion of the structure that stood in the way of his advance. Josephus' description says that the latest form of the Hasmonean Temple Mount had been adorned with porticoes (covered porches), an area that may be identified with "Solomon's Porch" (or "Colonnade") mentioned in the New Testament (John 10:23; Acts 3:11).[17] Josephus' reference to Herod's burning of Solomon's Porch relates to a colonnaded structure built on the eastern side of the Hasmonean Temple Mount. The name "Solomon's Porch" was apparently attached to the site because Solomon had originally built on the east side of the steep rocky hill, however, the portico that existed at the time of Herod's attack may have been a later addition, most likely from the Hellenistic period. Herod does not seem to have destroyed the entire structure, but only the front row of porticos, although it was not rebuilt until the reign of Herod Agrippa II (AD 48–93).

Herod secured his position as the proxy Jewish ruler under Roman occupation, dubbing himself "King Herod." Herod knew that in order to rule the Jewish people he would have to conform to traditional Jewish practices, so he converted to Judaism to appease the priests, and in 20 BC he proposed a renovation of the existing temple of Zerubbabel on a more magnificent scale.

By the time of Herod, the second temple had suffered centuries of assault, repairs, and the general ravages of time. In making plans to reconstruct the temple, Herod had to follow the biblical design and legal requirements that governed the size of the building he could construct. However, Herod had other parties to please, and most important of these were the Roman authorities upon whom his right to rule depended. If his architectural projects could make Jerusalem a modern metropolis rivaling other Roman cities with a magnificent building that highlighted the classical tastes of the West, he could hope to retain Roman favor.

Because many of the inhabitants of Jerusalem and other cities under Herod's rule were Hellenistic Jews, they were accustomed to classical culture that boasted temples and shrines on a massive scale. Therefore, Herod's motives in remodeling the temple were mixed at best, and history judges them as bittersweet. On one hand, rebuilding and enlarging the temple complex is considered one of Herod's major architectural accomplishments. On the other hand, Herod's intentions were to transform Jerusalem from a provincial Jewish community to a model of Hellenistic culture and to

THE HERODIAN DYNASTY

King Herod (73–4 BC) appears in the account of the Magi in Matthew 2, a time when the aged king was executing members of his family whom he feared might be plotting against him.

Upon King Herod's death, his son Archelaus inherited Judea. Herod Archelaus ruled Judea with an iron fist, quelling any disorder that broke out in Jerusalem. The Gospel of Matthew indicates that Archelaus's rule was the reason why, after leaving Egypt, Joseph and Mary settled in Nazareth in Galilee, and not Judea (Matthew 2:22).

King Herod's other son Antipas (shown above) was appointed ruler of Galilee. Herod Antipas is most often referred to in the Gospels simply as "Herod." He was responsible for John the Baptizer's execution (John 6:14–26) and Jesus was sent to him to stand trial because Jesus was from Galilee (Luke 23:6–12).

impress the Romans while appeasing the Jews. While the temple itself conformed to the divine design, other elements of the temple complex were clearly Greco-Roman in style, such as the Royal Stoa (Porch).

Even though Herod's rebuilding of the temple may have appeared to be an act of devotion to God, at this same time he also built a temple to the goddess Roma at Caesarea. His appointments to office of the high priest were also to suit his political aims. In 36 BC he named his 17-year-old son-in-law Aristobulus III as high priest (although murdering him the very next year), and in 23 BC he married the high priest Simon's daughter (his third wife, whom he also murdered).

When Roman custom and laws of Jewish sanctity came into conflict, Herod was quick to side with his Roman overlords. In one instance, he confiscated the high priest's vestments as a demonstration of superior (Roman) authority. In another show of loyalty to Rome, he installed a golden image of an eagle over the eastern entrance to the temple.[18] As a bird of prey, the eagle symbolized the character of Rome, and it corrupted the character of the temple as a place of peace. Because of this desecration, a riot occurred in 4 BC led by High Priest Matthias. A group of about 40 Jews tore down the hated image and hacked it to pieces. This defiant act on the Temple Mount resulted in the high priest's removal and his coactivists being burned alive.

Herod's son Archelaus, the year after his father's death in 4 BC, slaughtered about 3,000 Jewish nationalists in the temple at Passover. In the same year Jewish nationalists rioted and burned the temple cloisters (covered walkways). In AD 28, Pontius Pilate, the Roman-appointed governor over Judea, also engaged in an attack on and in the temple, taking money from the temple treasuries to construct an aqueduct, and then in the temple courts during a protest he massacred a number of Galilean zealots (Jewish rebels who wanted to oust the Romans; see Luke 13:1–2).

HELLENISM

Toward the end of the fourth century BC Alexander the Great spread Greek civilization to the lands he conquered in an attempt to create a universal Greek culture. The land of Israel came under Greek rule and the influence of Hellenism (from *hellas*, the Greek word for Greece). Jews who adopted Greek culture or who mixed it with the religion and traditions of Judaism were called Hellenistic Jews. On the positive side this movement produced the Greek translation of the Hebrew Bible known as the Septuagint, as well as Jewish apocryphal and apocalyptic literature which sought to develop Jewish

hopes and aspirations. However, orthodox Jewish sects opposed Hellenistic Jews, believing that the practice of Greek culture violated the Mosaic Law. This led in the second century BC to a revolt against Greek rule in Israel and to the formation of the Hasmonean Dynasty. Eventually, corruption in this rule coupled with a continued opposition to Hellenism led to Roman control of the country. Hellenistic Jews remained a part of the Jewish community, but were often ostracized by or disputed with by other Jewish groups, a problem faced by the early Jewish-Christian church (Acts 6:1; 9:29).

Temple

Antonia Fortress

Warren's
Gate

Wilson's
Arch

Barclay's
Gate

Shops

Mount of Olives

Solomon's Porch

Royal Stoa

Soreg

City Walls

Place of Trumpeting

Triple Gate

Double Gate

Robinson's Arch

Shops

Shops

Monumental Staircase

The Temple Mount, Jerusalem, First Century AD.
This painting shows the Herodian Temple Mount in the late afternoon near the end of the second temple period. The view looks east from the vantage point (left front) of the mansion of the High Priest Kathros (site of today's Jewish Quarter).

(Artist: Balage Balogh, Archaeology Illustrated.com)

Herod's Construction

The condition of the second temple and Herod's plans for a much larger structure included the complete dismantling of the old temple.[19] However, the priests did not trust Herod and feared that his call for a destruction of the existing structure was a ruse and that he was secretly staging an attack on the temple.[20] Therefore, Herod was required to prepare and transport all of the building stones for the new temple to the Temple Mount in the sight of the people before permission was given to touch a single stone of the previous structure.

It is unclear exactly how long the construction of the temple and sacrificial area took. Josephus says that the temple took a year and a half to complete and the stoa and the outer courts took eight years.[21] But also, according to the biblical record (John 2:20) and Josephus,[22] the temple complex was a continual work-in-progress until the Jewish Revolt broke out in AD 66.

THE TEMPLE

Herod added new compartments and a second story above the innermost chambers of the temple. These additions doubled the temple building in height and width. However, the size of the Holy of Holies itself may not have been changed because these dimensions were given by divine command and because it may have had to conform to the rock that protruded within the building, which restricted any alteration by Herod.

THE TEMPLE MOUNT

Herod also doubled the size of the Temple Mount and added massive new structures: the Antonia Fortress to the north of the Temple Mount and the Royal Stoa to the south. The Antonia Fortress served as military barracks for Roman soldiers. The Royal Stoa, the largest structure on the Temple Mount, was a common meeting place for those entering the temple complex. The Temple Mount, an extensive platform with huge retaining walls to

When Herod removed the old foundations of the second temple, he left the old eastern wall with its portico intact. This can be seen today on the outside of the eastern wall where a "seam" is visible near the southern corner. This seam (straight joint) separates the Hasmonean extension (53 ft; 16 m; stones to right of the seam) from the Herodian extension (105 ft; 32 m; stones to the left of the seam). The bend is the end of the eastern wall and the 500-cubit-square Temple Mount. In the middle is a long horizontal stone which is the remains of an arch. Just above it is a smaller stone which is the remains of an ancient double gate that led to Temple Mount storage vaults.

In the 1990s a tunnel was opened alongside the underground course of stones so that visitors could see the full extent of the Herodian construction. In the course exposed in this tunnel is one of the most massive of the foundation stones yet discovered. Its measurements are 45 feet (13.72 m) by 11 feet (3.35 m) by 14–16 feet (4.27–4.88 m) and it weighs nearly 600 tons.
(Baker Photo Archive)

bear the weight of the fill and of the structures to be built above, was trapezoidal in shape.[23] The total area of this sacred precinct was 172,000 square yards (144,000 square meters; approximately 35 acres). This made the Temple Mount the largest site of its kind in the ancient world. Its sacred area was twice as large as the monumental Forum Romanum built by Trajan, and three and a half times larger than the combined temples of Jupiter and Astarte-Venus at Baalbek.

To accomplish this feat, Herod's engineers had to construct enormous retaining (supporting) walls, many 15 feet (4.57 m) thick, with some towering more than 150 feet (45.72 m) from their bedrock foundation that sloped upward from the south to the north. The most famous remnant of these retaining walls standing today is known as the Western Wall (Wailing Wall; Hebrew, *Kotel*). The exposed walls are more than 1,500 feet (457 m) in length (north to south) and 900 feet (274 m) in width (east to west). Their height is about 50 feet (15 m) above the modern plaza, yet the course of stones in the southern end continues down another 50 feet (15 m). (See *Western Wall* on page 101.)

The Western Wall. The exposed portion of the Western Wall shown here is also called the "Wailing Wall" from the tradition that Jews came to this site to mourn the destruction of the temple. Today it is a special place of prayer for Jews and visitors to the Temple Mount.

THE WORKFORCE

The massive construction project required an equally massive workforce. For this Herod brought in 10,000 skilled workers. Since Jewish law required that only priests could construct the temple,[24] Herod employed 1,000 priests to serve as masons and carpenters. Herod also used the local population as workers; as they were under the supervision of the priests, they were made to conform to ritual regulations.

STONES FOR THE TEMPLE COMPLEX

In 2007 the rock quarry from which the priests got the stones used for the temple and its complex was discovered. Located in Jerusalem's ultra-orthodox neighborhood of Ramat Shlomo, the quarried stones each weighed about 20 tons. Stones this size had never been found in an archaeological excavation anywhere in the country, except in the walls of the Temple Mount. The use of such immense stones allowed construction without the need for cement or plaster, and maintained the stability of the structure of the walls of the Temple Mount for thousands of years.

The remains of this quarry also revealed how Herod's stonecutters had done the quarrying. Each stone block was prepared in the following stages:

- A deep, narrow channel was chiseled around all four sides of the block, isolating it from the surrounding bedrock surface.

- A row of cleaving stakes was inserted in the bottom part of the block until a fissure was created and the stone was detached. This was accomplished by driving logs of wood into the channels and pouring water on the wood to make it swell, exerting lateral pressure on the block and splitting it from the bedrock.

- Stonemasons dressed the rough blocks with margins on their outer faces to produce an ashlar (a finished stone block), but left projections on opposite sides of the blocks so ropes could be lashed around the projections.

- A crane would hoist one end of the ashlar block off the ground and lower it onto a wooden roller. The construction area was 125 feet (38.1 m) lower than the quarry in the north, so the ashlar blocks could be easily hauled down to the site area where the wall was to be built. Getting the ashlars in place was accomplished by use of a treadmill-powered crane.

Ashlars of the Temple Complex (Author in photo)

Winch device for raising ashlars

The New Temple Mount: Porches, Gates, and Courts

THE PORCHES (STOAS)

The Royal Stoa

At the southern end of his extended platform, Herod built a monumental multi-storied basilica called the Royal Stoa or Royal Portico (Porch). This was the largest structure on the Temple Mount, stretching across almost the entire length of the southern wall from east to west, and was praised by Josephus as one "more deserving of mention than any other under the sun."[25] This magnificent roofed pavilion was sustained by 162 pillars, each 50 feet (15 m) high and 16 feet (4.87 m) in circumference, arranged in four rows and topped with Corinthian capitals.[26] People would enter the Stoa by a long set of monumental steps that ascended from the lowest point in the Kidron Valley near the Pool of Siloam and led worshipers up to the Huldah gates and through two underground passageways up onto the Temple Mount.

The Royal Stoa served as a common meeting place and led to the large open Court of the Gentiles, one of Herod's additions on the southern side. It was said that the scribes held their schools in the colonnades and that rabbis, such as Rabbi Gamaliel, taught near the Royal Stoa. At the eastern end the Stoa, the Sanhedrin (the supreme court of Israel) convened their daily meetings.

Passover in Herod's Temple, First Century AD. This painting shows a view from inside the Royal Stoa looking north toward the temple. Note the colorful appearance of the columns and roof of the Royal Stoa. The use of such colors on all of the buildings of the temple complex has been verified by both documentary and archaeological evidence. (Artist: Balage Balogh, Archaeology Illustrated.com)

The Stoa of Solomon (Solomon's Porch)

The eastern portion of the wall with its single-story roofed colonnades was called the Stoa of Solomon or Solomon's Porch. Its pre-Herodian status can be confirmed archaeologically since the Herodian additions on the north and south of the wall were built to conform to this structure. For some reason, it was believed that Solomon had originally built this porch, and Herod himself may have also believed this (or at least accepted the popular notion) because he did not alter it in his architectural expansion.

Solomon's Porch in the New Testament:

- John 10:22–23 states that Jesus walked in Solomon's Porch and had a confrontation with a Jewish crowd there during the Feast of Dedication (Hanukkah).
- Acts 3:11 refers to this area as the place to which the crowd ran to see the lame man healed through Peter and John. This may imply that this was the particular place where the early church assembled (Acts 2:46–47).

Remains of Robinson's Arch

Robinson's Arch, First Century AD. This painting depicts a street level view from the southwestern corner below the Herodian Temple Mount. The vaulted walkway, known today as Robinson's Arch, frames the paved open-air pedestrian street lined with shops that ran the full length along the western side of the Temple Mount.

(Artist: Balage Balogh, Archaeology Illustrated.com)

THE RED HEIFER

The red heifer ceremony (Numbers 19) was conducted on the Mount of Olives where a heifer of three years of age was burnt and its ashes transported along a wooden bridge over the Kidron ravine to a repository near the East Gate of the Temple Mount. After the destruction of the second temple in AD 70, this repository of red heifer ashes disappeared, as did red heifers themselves.

The red heifer ceremony was done for ritual cleansing (restoration from corpse impurity). The 113th of the 613 mandatory commandments in Judaism states, "the ashes of the Red Heifer are to be used in the process of ritual purification." Without a purified priesthood the work of consecrating the site and rebuilding the temple cannot begin. This explains why Jewish organizations desiring to rebuild the temple today have sought to reinstitute the red heifer ceremony. Orthodox Jewish Rabbi Chaim Richman explains, "In truth, the fate of the entire world depends on the Red Heifer. For God has ordained that its ashes alone is the single missing ingredient for the reinstatement of Biblical purity—and thereafter, the rebuilding of the Holy Temple."[30]

GATES

There were both exterior entrances that led from the city to the Temple Mount as well as interior entrances that led into the temple precincts. These gates were not simply openings in a wall, but were large two- and three-story structures having a central passageway with rooms on either side.

The Outer Gates [27]

Four gates on the western side:

- Robinson's Arch
- Barclay's Gate
- Wilson's Arch
- Warren's Gate

One gate on the northern side:

- The Tadi Gate

Three gates on the eastern side:

- A southeastern bridge (like Robinson's Arch)
- The Miphkad Gate
- The Eastern or Shushan Gate (near the present-day Golden Gate)

Two gates on the southern side:

- The Double Gate and Triple Gate (The Huldah Gates)

The Eastern (Shushan) Gate

The eastern and southern gates were the most prominent. The Eastern Gate was called the Shushan (or Susa) Gate because it bore a relief of the Shushan Palace in Babylon.[28] Contrary to popular opinion, the Shushan Gate was not a public entrance or exit, but was used on Yom Kippur (Day of Atonement) for leading the scapegoat into the wilderness. The Miphkad Gate was used exclusively for the red heifer ceremony, but the Eastern Gate was used by the priests going in and out of the temple to perform this ceremony that took place on the Mt. of Olives, opposite this gate across the Kidron Valley. The Mishnah says that a wooden causeway was built from the Mt. of Olives to this gate especially for this unique ceremony (Num. 19).[29]

The Eastern Gate. (Messiah in the Temple Foundation)

Herod's Temple: Outer Gates and Porches

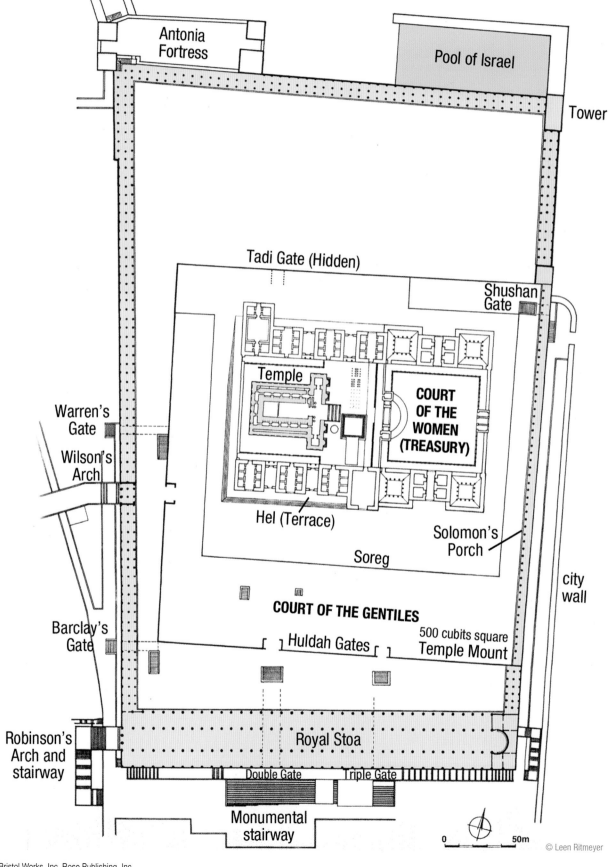

Antonia Fortress

Pool of Israel

Tower

Tadi Gate (Hidden)

Shushan Gate

Temple

COURT OF THE WOMEN (TREASURY)

Warren's Gate

Wilson's Arch

Hel (Terrace)

Solomon's Porch

Soreg

city wall

COURT OF THE GENTILES

Barclay's Gate

Huldah Gates

500 cubits square Temple Mount

Robinson's Arch and stairway

Royal Stoa

Double Gate

Triple Gate

Monumental stairway

0   50m

© Leen Ritmeyer

The Double and Triple Gates

The most popular entrance to the temple was from the south through the Double and Triple Gates which led onto the Temple Mount and in through the Huldah Gates. The Huldah Gates were likely named after the first temple period prophetess who held court in this area. The Double Gate was situated on the west side of the southern wall and was for the people. Some scholars suggest that this is the gate the New Testament refers to as the "Beautiful Gate" (Acts 3:2, 10). The Triple Gate, on the east side of the southern wall and located 215 feet (65.5 m) from the Double Gate, was for the priests.

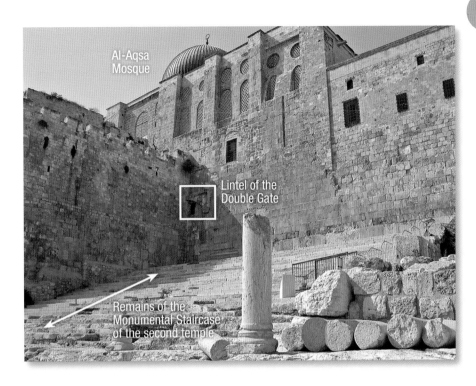

Al-Aqsa Mosque

Lintel of the Double Gate

Remains of the Monumental Staircase of the second temple

The Monumental Staircase

One of the impressive sights to those visiting the Temple Mount was a grand staircase that gave access from the southern side of the city leading to the Double and Triple Gate entrances. These steps began at the Pool of Siloam located far to the south deep within the Kidron Valley. The steps alternate between long and short steps. The steps ended once worshipers reached the southern entrance to the Temple Mount and entered through the Double and Triple Gates. The width of the steps leading to the Double Gate was 213 feet (65 m) and the width of the steps leading to the Triple Gate was 51 feet (15.5 m).

The Inner Gates

The interior entrances to the temple precincts were massive gates 52 feet (15.8 m) high and 26 feet (8 m) wide with two doors, and overlaid with silver and gold:

- The Nicanor Gate (from the Court of Women to the Court of the Israelites)
- The Southern Gate (to the Court of the Women)
- The Water Gate (leading to the area of the laver)
- The Gate of the Firstborn (leading to the altar of burnt offering)
- The Kindling/Fuel Gate (leading to rear of the temple)
- The Northern Gate (leading to the Court of the Women)
- The Gate of the Flame/Song (leading to the Court of the Priests)
- The Gate of the Offering (leading to the Temple Court)
- The Gate of Jeconiah (the gate furthest west near the Chamber of the Hearth)

STREET SHOPS

In the archaeological excavations at the southern wall, a fragment of a ritual vessel inscribed with the Hebrew word *qorban* ("[dedicated] offering") and a drawing of two pigeons was found on the paved Herodian street. This provides evidence that in the time of Jesus, the commerce of the street shops had found its way into the Royal Stoa where Jesus encountered the moneychangers and those selling animals (John 2:14–16).

THE COURTS

Josephus provides a description of the temple's four courts with guidelines based on ritual restrictions about who was allowed to enter.[31] These courts from east to west increased in degree of sanctity. The outer Court of the Gentiles, as the name implies, was open to all—men or women, Jew or non-Jew—except the ceremonially unclean. The next court, the Court of the Women, was open to Jewish men and all ritually clean Jewish women. The next court, the Court of the Israelites, was restricted to Jewish men. The closest court to the temple was the Court of the Priests which was the most sacred court[32] and only priests on duty could enter it. According to Josephus, an extremely high and thick wall surrounded the outer courts.[33] (See *Ritually Clean* on page 81.)

The Court of the Gentiles

The expansive Court of the Gentiles sported a popular bazaar underneath the protective roof of the Royal Stoa. Here moneychangers exchanged local coinage for the pure silver Tyrian shekel so that a proper offering could be made to the temple. (The Tyrian shekel was required because Roman currency was defiling and the Romans forbid the Jews to coin their own money.) Here, too, vendors sold animals for use as burnt offerings.

This market was still considered *inside* the temple complex, even though it was removed from the actual temple precincts. For example, John 7:28 says that Jesus "cried out in the temple," although the text locates him in the area of the temple treasury within the Court of the Women (John 8:20). Although the next court after the Court of the Gentiles, this court was still outside the area of greater sanctity (since lepers could enter here). This helps us understand Jesus' concern over the sanctity of the temple at his entrance to the Royal Stoa situated on the threshold of the Temple Court (Matthew 21:13). It also explains why his clash with the temple vendors was a fairly modest incident, permitting his daily return to the temple precincts to address the crowds (Luke 19:47). If it had occurred in the more public open area of the Court of the Gentiles, it would have been considered not just a religious demonstration, but also a political threat, and he would have been arrested.

The Court of the Gentiles was the only non-Jewish access to the Temple Mount. To prevent unauthorized trespass into the sacred courts, the area on the far south and west was bounded by a paved terrace on top of a stairway. A stone fence, the *soreg*, served as the main barrier which Gentiles and the ceremonially unclean were forbidden to pass.[34] According to Josephus, it stood 5 feet 2 inches (1.57 m) high. To insure this boundary was not improperly breached, large stone inscriptions in Greek and Latin that threatened death to violators were posted at each entrance to the courts.

Soreg Inscription. First-century warning in Greek to Gentiles to avoid areas of the temple that were off limits under pentalty of death. It reads, "No foreigner shall enter within the balustrade of the temple and whoever shall be caught shall be responsible for his own death that will follow in consequence [of] his trespassing."

Archaeological excavations uncovered numerous ritual immersion pools (*miqva'ot*) as part of a public bathhouse located between the steps leading up to the Court of the Gentiles. These were probably the pools used to baptize the 3,000 converts on the Day of Pentecost in Acts 2. Crowds of pilgrims coming to the temple for the Feast of Pentecost would have entered by the southern entrance through the Double Gate into the Royal Stoa and congregated in the Court of the Gentiles. Apparently, the disciples of Jesus (as many as 120) had gathered with this crowd (Acts 2:1). When the Holy Spirit descended and filled these disciples, the rest of the crowd took notice, heard the preaching of Peter, and those who believed were baptized, likely at this nearby bathhouse. Numerous immersion pools were located within this bathhouse and this structure was the most convenient for baptizing, being located between the Huldah Gates on the southern steps.

Herod's Temple: Inner Gates and Courts

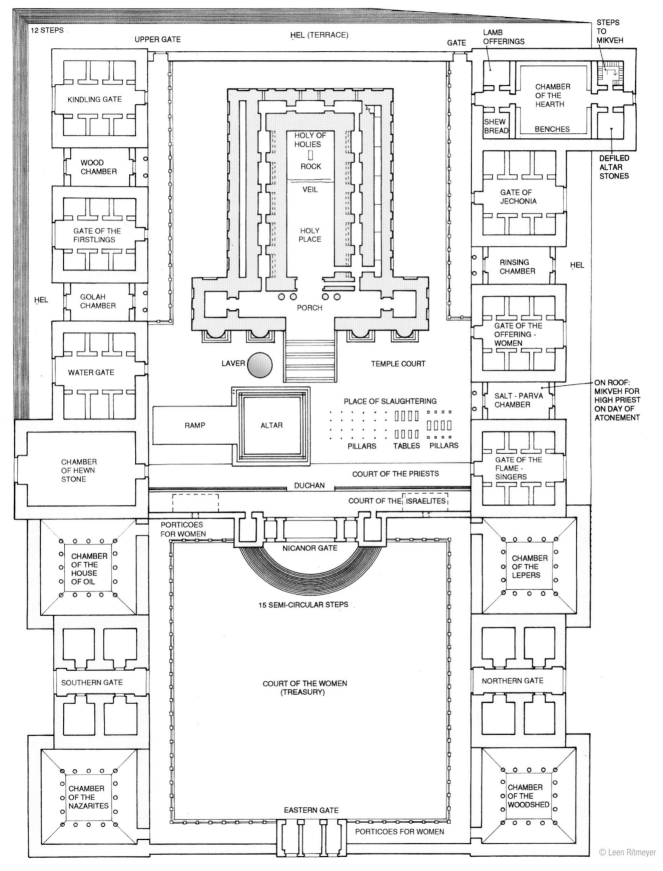

12 STEPS

UPPER GATE   HEL (TERRACE)   GATE   LAMB OFFERINGS   STEPS TO MIKVEH

KINDLING GATE   CHAMBER OF THE HEARTH

SHEW BREAD   BENCHES

WOOD CHAMBER   DEFILED ALTAR STONES

HOLY OF HOLIES
ROCK
VEIL
HOLY PLACE

GATE OF JECHONIA

GATE OF THE FIRSTLINGS

HEL   GOLAH CHAMBER   PORCH   RINSING CHAMBER   HEL

WATER GATE   GATE OF THE OFFERING - WOMEN

LAVER   TEMPLE COURT

ON ROOF: MIKVEH FOR HIGH PRIEST ON DAY OF ATONEMENT

SALT - PARVA CHAMBER

PLACE OF SLAUGHTERING

RAMP   ALTAR

PILLARS   TABLES   PILLARS

GATE OF THE FLAME - SINGERS

CHAMBER OF HEWN STONE

COURT OF THE PRIESTS

DUCHAN

COURT OF THE ISRAELITES

PORTICOES FOR WOMEN

CHAMBER OF THE HOUSE OF OIL   NICANOR GATE   CHAMBER OF THE LEPERS

15 SEMI-CIRCULAR STEPS

SOUTHERN GATE   NORTHERN GATE

COURT OF THE WOMEN (TREASURY)

CHAMBER OF THE NAZARITES   CHAMBER OF THE WOODSHED

EASTERN GATE

PORTICOES FOR WOMEN

© Leen Ritmeyer

The Court of the Women

The Court of the Women, the largest of the courts, was a square courtyard measuring 233 feet (71 m) on each side (a football field is 360 feet long). Some scholars estimate that at the time of the feasts it could have held 6,000 worshipers at one time. It was not only open to ceremonially purified Jewish women, but also to ritually impure priests, Nazirites, and even lepers.

The walls of this court were lined with porticoes that formed a corridor from east to west and held four unroofed chambers (smaller rooms attached to and within the main structure).

- **The Chamber of the Nazirites** in the southeast corner was the place where those under the Nazirite vow cut their hair and cooked their peace offerings.

- **The Chamber of the Lepers** in the northwest corner was where lepers ritually immersed themselves before presenting themselves to the priest for inspection (Leviticus 14:1–7). In Matthew 8:4, after healing a leper, Jesus told him to go show himself to the priest and to make the prescribed thank offering.

- **The Chamber of the House of Oil** in the southwest corner stored the wine and oil for drink offerings and grain offerings along with the menorah (lampstands).[35]

- **The Chamber of the Woodshed** in the northeast corner was the place where unclean priests were employed inspecting firewood to be used on the altar of burnt offering.

It was said that this court was often filled with singing and dancing. One occasion when such a celebration occurred in this court was the annual water-drawing ceremony when a priest drew spring water from the Pool of Siloam and carried it to the temple to pour on the altar. This ceremony took place during the conclusion of the annual celebration of the Feast of Tabernacles (Booths), and its purpose in this act was to ask God to send rain which was necessary for a successful harvest. It was on this last day of the Feast of Tabernacles that Jesus taught in the Court of the Women saying, "Let anyone who is thirsty come to me and drink" and "rivers of living water will flow from within them" (John 7:37–39). Jesus was speaking about the outpouring of the Holy Spirit—the promise associated with the Messiah's coming—which like the rain, depended on the proper response from Israel.

In each of the four corners of the Court of the Women stood two immense *menorot* (lampstands). These were lit day and night, especially at festival occasions such as the Feast of Tabernacles. During this festival, Jesus took the opportunity, while these majestic lampstands were still lit, to point to his own messianic purpose to be "the light of the world" (John 8:12).

The Roman historian Tacitus declared that the temple "possessed enormous riches."[36] These riches were stored in the temple treasury, which held everything designated for or donated to the temple.[37] The temple treasury was located in the Court of the Women. According to the Mishnah, somewhere in the Court of the Women were 13 wooden boxes for collecting contributions that would be deposited through bronze trumpet-shaped receptacles.[38]

The Gospel of Luke says that when Jesus and his disciples

The Widow's Offering. (Painting by James Tissot)

RITUALLY CLEAN

Ritual cleanliness was an important concept in Bible times. In the Old Testament, God chose Israel to be separate ("holy") from the other nations. As such, his people had to maintain a level of sanctity. Israel's cleanliness laws reflected the necessity of respecting the holiness of God who had chosen them.

People could become unclean in a number of ways: for example, having a skin disease, eating certain foods, or touching a carcass. Some of these things were associated with death (the consequence of sin), but the association of others (such as the dietary laws) are less clear. Nevertheless, they were violations of sanctity because God revealed them as such. In the temple complex, the closer a person got to the location of God's presence, the higher the requirements for holiness or cleanliness. People who had become unclean could be restored by undergoing various rituals and waiting for a set period of time.

The cleanliness laws pictured how human falleness separates humanity from a holy God. Respecting the cleanliness laws showed respect for God's holiness and his commands. These laws impressed on the mind of every Israelite the sacredness of God and his high standards. (See Mark 7:1–23 for Jesus' discussion on cleanliness.)

were in the area of the "temple treasury," Jesus watched both the rich and poor depositing their contributions (Luke 21:1). He drew to the disciples' attention a widow who had deposited two copper coins into one of the trumpets. Jesus used her example to teach that when the poor give they give more than the rich because they give out of their poverty, while the rich give from their abundance (Luke 21:2–4).

When Judas threw "into the temple" the 30 pieces of silver (Tyrian half-shekels) paid to him by the Sanhedrin for betraying Jesus, he created a dilemma for the chief priest. Even though this money had been deposited in the temple it was considered the price of a life ("blood money"), so the chief priest stated it could not be deposited into the temple treasury (Matthew 27:3–6).

The Court of the Israelites

The Court of the Israelites was limited to ritually pure Jewish men. It was entered by the curved staircase leading up to the Nicanor Gate. This court consisted of a narrow hall 233 feet (71 m) wide and 19 feet (5.8 m) deep. Beneath this court were rooms that opened into the lower Court of the Women. These were used for storing musical instruments and equipment used by the Levites.[39]

The Temple Court (Court of the Priests)

Some scholars understand the Court of the Priests as including the temple, its installations, and the buildings and storerooms associated with the priestly duties. Others see it as having the same dimensions as the Court of the Israelites—actually one long hall, which is why it is referred to in the Mishnah as the "Hall of Priests"[40]—and that there was a separate Temple Court (Hebrew *Azarah*). If there was indeed a separate Temple Court, this Court of Priests seems to have been a sacred space separating the Court of the Israelites from the Temple Court, which only priests could enter.

The Temple Court was the court of greatest sanctity and importance because it included the temple itself. In the Temple Court stood the altar of burnt offering, the place of slaughtering, the laver, and the temple.[41]

Three Chambers on the South Side of the Temple Court:
* **The Pen of Wood** (also called the "Wood Chamber"). In this chamber, the good wood used for the altar was separated from the moldy wood.
* **The Golah Chamber.** This chamber served as an office for the exile[42] and had a water wheel to draw water from the Golah Cistern.[43] This chamber's name reveals that it had some relationship to those Jews who had returned from exile (Hebrew *golah*) in Babylon.
* **The Water Gate**: This is the chamber where the temple's vast underground water supply was controlled.

Chambers on the North Side of the Temple Court: (east to west)

- **The Salt-Parvah Chamber(s)**: This chamber is where salt used in the sacrificial offerings was kept and where the skins from the sacrifices were salted down. It is uncertain if there was one or several salt-parvah chambers.

- **The Rinsing Chamber**: This chamber is where the slaughtered animal parts for the sacrifice were washed (probably the entrails).

- **The Chamber of the Hearth**: This chamber contained a large fire where off-duty priests could warm themselves. It had a domed roof and functioned as sleeping quarters for the priests. It also contained the Chamber of the Lambs where animals being readied for sacrifice were housed and could be inspected for disqualifying blemishes. It also contained a chamber associated with the offering of the showbread (bread of the presence).

The Laver

The biblical instructions in Exodus 30:17–21 required that the laver (Hebrew *kiyyor*) in the Temple Court be made of copper or brass (this included its base). The function of this washbasin was for the ritual purification of the priests who would serve in the daily sacrificial service. According to the biblical command, it was to be placed between the altar and the sanctuary and be filled with water. The priests were to wash their hands and feet in it to prepare for presenting burnt offerings on the altar or entering the temple. This was done by allowing water from faucets set into the laver to run over their hands and feet while holding their feet with their hands. Thus, this vessel was the first of the service vessels to be used each morning by the priests. The Mishnah speaks about a wooden device designed by a priest named Ben Katin which seems to have been a waterwheel mechanism that drew water for filling the laver from a large underground cistern.[45] According to these sources, the sound of this device in operation could be heard as far as the city of Jericho (located some 20 miles away; 32 km). The use of this waterwheel in the early morning officially began the priestly service in the Temple Court.

The Altar of Burnt Offering

After purification, the priest would walk up the altar of burnt offering by a ramp. On each corner of the altar were four projections called "horns." In the water-drawing ceremony during the Feast of Tabernacles, priests would pour water on these horns. There was a ledge called the "circuit," that defined the area in which the priests had to walk when offering the sacrifices. In the southwest corner of the circuit were two holes that served as a drainage system for removing the blood from the court.[46] Both Jesus and Paul referred to this altar of burnt offering and recognized its sanctity (Matthew 23:18–20; 1 Corinthians 9:13; 10:18).

The Place of Slaughtering

On the north side of the Temple Court were rows of 24 rings affixed to four rows of six short pillars set in the ground.[47] This was the site for the ritual slaughtering of animals used for the sacrifices. The rings were used to hold the animal in place. Slaughtering was a humane process that followed strict guidelines, including the catching of the animal's blood in a gold vessel.

THE PEN OF WOOD AND THE ARK

According to a story from the second temple, a priest serving in the "wood store" noticed some stones in the floor were different and surmised that a stone had once been removed and then replaced in order to hide the ark. When he went to announce that he had discovered the secret chamber of the ark, he was struck dead "lest he revealed the hiding place of the ark." On the basis of this account, Jewish tradition has held that the ark and other artifacts have all been hidden within a secret compartment beneath the Pen of Wood.[44]

Pictured at the bottom center is the Court of the Women with the great lampstands that burned day and night and the bronze Nicanor Gate opened and looking into the Court of the Priests. Rising beyond and above this court is the front of the holy temple with its golden façade and marble columns. (Messiah in the Temple Foundation)

The Temple

THE OUTER DESIGN

The magnificent sanctuary built by Herod faced east according to the biblical precedent. To pilgrims approaching from the Mt. of Olives, the temple's white-polished limestone and imported marble gave it the appearance of a great snow-clad mountain. The sight of the temple for anyone waking in the city was of a golden mountain as its limestone absorbed the morning rays of the sun. Once the sun had fully risen, the temple glowed with brilliance because the upper exterior of the building was covered with gold, which would reflect the sun. Josephus observed, that Herod adorned the outside of the temple with so much gold that when the sun shined on it, it blinded those who looked at it.[48]

Set on a 10-foot (3.05 m) thick foundation, the temple was 172 feet (52.43 m) in height. Josephus says it was wider in front and narrower behind.[49] This structure bore golden spikes each 21 inches (53.3 cm) in height whose purpose was to keep birds from congregating on the edge of the roof and despoiling the temple's beautiful facade.[50]

Decorated Limestone from the Second Temple

Approaching the temple from the west of the altar, a staircase of 12 steps ascended upward 10 feet from the floor of the Temple Court to the outer porch (Hebrew *ulam*) of the temple.[51] The porch was well known in the ancient world and was mentioned by the Roman historian Tacitus.[52] The porch was 15.6 feet (4.75 m) high and had to support the weight of the 88 feet (26.82 m) of courses of stone above it. (A "course" is the line of stones in a part of the wall, one above the other.) It had a decorated door with an inlaid shell motif over it; above this were four ornamented windows. Free standing posts (or pillars) and their lintel framing the door were adorned with an exquisite golden vine at least 34 feet (10.36 m) in length with leaves and hanging grape clusters "as tall as a man."[53] However, Josephus' description of the doorways and veils has been interpreted by scholars in two ways: the golden vine adorned the temple pillars, or the golden vine was woven into the veil itself.

Around the outside of the inner sanctuary (Holy Place and Holy of Holies) were 38 small chambers built in three stories.[54] These chambers formed a honeycomb structure and may have contributed to structural support in the architecture. These chambers were probably for storing temple vessels, utensils, vestments, and other supplies.

THE HOLY PLACE

Moving westward through the porch one entered the Holy Place (Hebrew *Heikal*), the sacred space exclusive to priestly service before the Holy of Holies. It was said that Queen Helena of Adiabene donated a golden lamp that hung over the entrance whose inner walls were overlaid with gold.[55] Separating the porch and the Holy Place was a set of double folding doors (one on the outside and one on the inside) that folded back on themselves so that one side fit neatly into a recess in the wall.[56] These massive doors were covered by an equally massive curtain (the outer veil) which Josephus describes as a Babylonian tapestry 60 feet (18.29 m) high and 30 feet (9.14 m) wide and a "handbreadth" thick (3–4 in.; 8–10 cm).[57] The curtain was so heavy that it was said to have taken 300 priests to immerse it when it became unclean.[58] (However, this description might not have been intended to be taken literally, but was rather an exaggerated way of speaking to emphasize how massive the curtain was.)

Cross Section of Herod's Temple

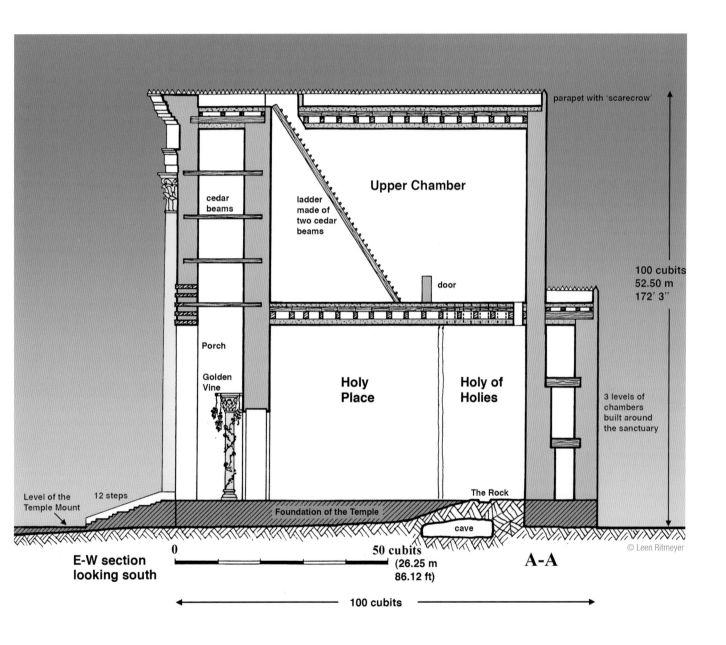

Upper Chamber

cedar beams

ladder made of two cedar beams

door

Porch

Golden Vine

Holy Place

Holy of Holies

The Rock

Level of the Temple Mount

12 steps

Foundation of the Temple

cave

parapet with 'scarecrow'

100 cubits
52.50 m
172' 3"

3 levels of chambers built around the sanctuary

© Leen Ritmeyer

E-W section looking south

0

50 cubits
(26.25 m
86.12 ft)

A-A

100 cubits

The Holy Place itself was 68.8 feet (21 m) in length and 34.4 feet (10.5 m) in width and all of its walls were overlaid with gold. It contained the sacred vessels (furniture) for the priestly service, the golden lampstand (Hebrew *menorah*), the table of the bread of the presence (Hebrew *shulchan hama'reket*) and the golden altar of incense (Hebrew *mizbach haketoret*).[59] Josephus describes the lampstand as "made of gold but constructed on a different pattern from those we use in ordinary life. Affixed to a pedestal was a central shaft, from which there extended slender branches, arranged trident-fashion, a wrought lamp being attached to the extremity of each branch; of these there were seven, indicating the honor paid to the number among the Jews."[60] The New Testament records that Zechariah, the father of John the Baptizer, was chosen by lot to perform the service at the altar of incense within the temple (Luke 1:11).

Ancient Assyrian depiction of a cherub

THE HOLY OF HOLIES (MOST HOLY PLACE)

The Holy of Holies (Hebrew *qodesh haqqodashim*) was technically known as the *Devir*. No part of the sanctuary had greater sanctity than this small square room 34.4 feet (10.5 m) in length and breadth and 69 feet (21 m) in height. While the priests served within the Holy Place, no one but the high priest, and only on one day—the Day of Atonement—was allowed to enter into the Holy of Holies. Following the biblical precedent (Ezra 5:15), the priestly workmen had built the temple with the Holy of Holies in the exact same location as the previous two structures: over the bedrock platform (an exposed portion of Mt. Moriah) known as the "Foundation Stone."

The Inner Veil

A veil (Hebrew *paroket*) separated the Holy of Holies from the Holy Place.[61] According to the Mishnah, 82 young girls made the veil. Seventy-two individual sections were joined together. Its overall dimensions were 69 feet (21 m) high and 34 feet (10.36 m) wide and one handbreadth thick (3–4 in.; 8–10 cm).[62] However, the Mishnah also describes this veil as a double construction with more than 1.5 feet (half a meter) between the two curtains.[63] The first-century philosopher Philo called the outer curtain the "covering" and the inner curtain the "veil."[64] Hebrews 9:3 mentions a "second veil," but this probably refers only to the veil before the Holy of Holies and not the curtain before the Holy Place. From the Mishnah account, the high priest who entered the Holy of Holies from the Holy Place on the Day of Atonement passed between these two curtains. Once he reached the north side, he then turned around and went south with the curtain on his left hand until he came to the place of the ark where he was to place the fire pan and sprinkle the atoning blood.

THE "EMPTY" TEMPLE

Jewish tradition held that the ark of the covenant was hidden in one of the underground chambers beneath the Holy of Holies, but within the actual building itself, there was nothing.[70] The absence of any representation of the deity or an image of any kind in the temple was thought incredible throughout the ancient world. Its absence also set the Jewish temple apart from all others. In fact, this single detail was most mentioned in foreign accounts concerning the Jewish people and their sanctuary. This fact also explains the conflict encountered with the Jews when Roman emperor worship became popular and emperors sought to place statues in the temple as a sign of local devotion. Josephus tells of a compromise in which the Jews would offer a sacrifice in honor of the emperor instead of his image being placed in the Holy of Holies.[71]

THE ROCK

Inside the present-day Muslim Dome of the Rock shrine is a large stone (*as-Sakhra*). Archaeological architect Leen Ritmeyer believes that a square incised indentation in the surface of that stone may be the exact place where the ark of the covenant was once set. The indentation was there in order to prevent the ark from movement when the high priest used its poles to direct his approach to the mercy seat in the time of the first temple. The photograph here is from a view looking directly down upon the large rock in the center of the Dome of the Rock.

To understand why the Holy of Holies was so protected, it is necessary to consider that the room was not designed for humans, but for the invisible God. For that reason, the Holy of Holies was a windowless room so no one could see in. This, however, does not mean the room was not ornamented. Gold plates one cubit square (and thought to have been engraved with images of the cherubim) were hung on the walls of the room so that the entire room was overlaid with gold.[65] To emphasize further that this room was unapproachable, the high priest carried a fire pan with burning incense, which produced a thick smoke that completely filled the room (Leviticus 16:12–14). This was to be done before the high priest could approach the place of the ark. This act further enforced the separation from the Holy One, whose divine presence was localized in the innermost part of the Holy of Holies at the place of the ark. According to some traditions, it was said that the priests outside in the Holy Place held the ends of a rope attached to the high priest's ankle. The rope was attached in order to remove the priest's body from the Holy of Holies should he die or be slain while performing his duty on the Day of Atonement.[66]

The Foundation Stone

Like the first temple, the second temple was built so that the Holy of Holies enclosed an exposed protrusion of Mt. Moriah. Abraham had brought Isaac to this mountain according to God's command to offer him as a burnt offering (Genesis 22:1–24). Also, King David built an altar to the Lord on this mountain on the threshing floor of Araunah in gratitude for the preservation of Jerusalem (2 Samuel 24:21–25; 1 Chronicles 21:18–28). At the time of the first temple's dedication, the ark of the covenant had been installed on a stone platform built over this bedrock three fingerbreadths high.[67] Because the *shekinah* had descended to the ark upon this place, even though it later departed, this site acquired a special sanctity unlike any other spot on earth (1 Kings 8:6–11; Ezekiel 8:4; 11:23).

However, the ark had been removed before the destruction of the first temple and was never returned to its place. Therefore, Josephus states that in the Herodian second temple "nothing whatsoever" stood in the Holy of Holies.[68] The Talmud explains that "after the ark was taken away a stone remained there from the time of the early Prophets, and it was called *shetiyah*. It was higher than the ground by three fingerbreadths. On this he [the high priest] used to put (the fire-pan)."[69] The Hebrew term used today for this barren stone is *'Even Ha-Shetiyah* ("the Foundation Stone"), on which Jewish tradition says, during the Day of Atonement the high priest would sprinkle the sacrificial blood at the place where the ark with its mercy seat had stood.

Herod's Temple Cutaway

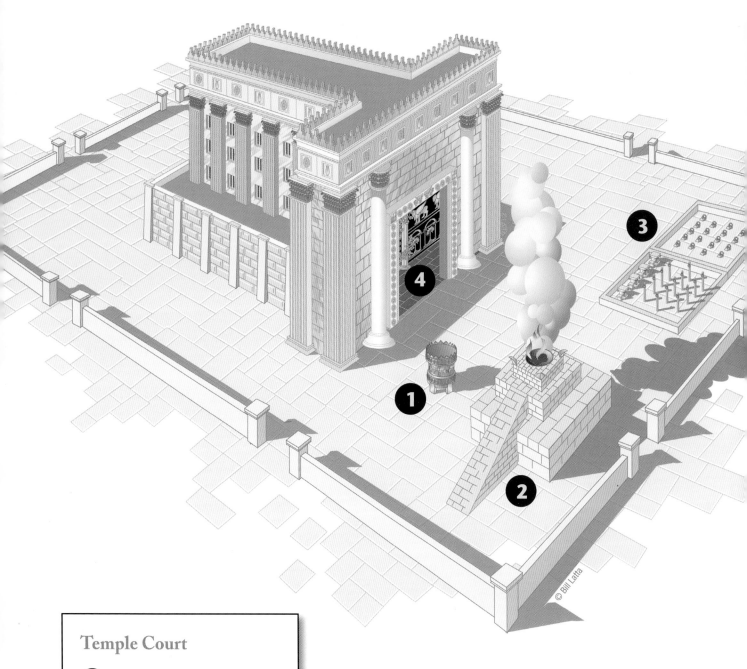

© Bill Latta

Temple Court

1 The Brazen Laver

2 The Altar of Burnt Offering

3 The Place Slaughtering

4 The Porch of the Temple

© Bill Latta

The Holy Place

5 Double-Folding Doors and Outer Veil

6 The Golden Lampstand (Menorah)

7 The Table of Showbread

8 The Golden Altar of Incense

The Holy of Holies (Most Holy Place)

9 The Inner Veil

10 The Foundation Stone

11 Chambers of the Inner Sanctuary

The Temple's Importance in the Time of Jesus

THE JEWISH PEOPLE

Despite the fact that the second temple had been constructed by Herod the Great, the Jewish people looked to the Jerusalem temple as the legitimate, central sanctuary of the God of Israel and the only place to which prayers could be directed and sacrifices offered. Even Jews in the Diaspora (Jewish communities in lands outside Israel) sent tithes to support the temple service. Positive references to the temple are found even in Hellenistic writings such as Ben Sirach, *Letter of Aristeas* and Philo of Alexandria.[72]

However, there were also rival sects of Judaism (both in the Hasmonean and Roman periods) that came into conflict over the qualifications of priests, how the priests should perform their duties, and how to respond to offenses made against the temple by Roman officials. For this reason some Jews believed that the second temple had been defiled[73] and was doomed to be destroyed and replaced by a purer third temple that conformed to the restoration ideal of the prophets.[74] Some even drew up blueprints for a replacement temple. (See *Temple Scroll* on page 136.)

PHARISEES AND SADDUCEES: WHAT'S THE DIFFERENCE?

The Pharisees and the Sadducees were religious groups during the second temple period.

- The Pharisees "separated" (Hebrew *parush* from which the term "Pharisee" is derived) from other groups who had accepted the Hasmonean control of the offices of king and high priest and those groups who assimilated with Hellenism (pro-Greek culture). They were religious conservatives who promoted Oral Law and were regarded as experts in legal interpretation. For this reason they were often called rabbi ("my teacher"). They also held that all Jews should observe the laws of ritual purity (associated with the temple service) outside the temple and even in times where foreign rule forced assimilation to pagan practices.

- The Sadducees (Hebrew *seduqim* "just/right ones") were a priestly group that arose from the Judean aristocracy and had a dominant role in society, politics, and religion. As the temple was the center of society, their primary status as priests connected them with the temple and gave them control over its various institutions and services.

Pharisees and Sadducees differed from one another socially and politically. This often brought them into conflict. Sadducees, as priests with power, were supported by the wealthy aristocrats, whereas the Pharisees were favored by the common people. The Sadducees tolerated Hellenism while the Pharisees opposed it. The Sadducees emphasized the importance of the temple, whereas the Pharisees emphasized the importance of other Mosaic laws. The Sadducees recognized only the Written Torah and rejected supernatural activity, angelic beings, and the concept of resurrection, while the Pharisees accepted all of these, adopting the Oral Law in addition to the biblical texts. The Sadducees disappeared after the destruction of the temple in AD 70, but the Pharisees came through it and emerged in the form of the rabbinical authorities.

THE LIFE AND MINISTRY OF JESUS

Most of the events in Jesus' earthly ministry occurred largely within a Jewish context and during a time when Herod's temple was functioning. It is interesting to consider how much of Jesus' ministry and teaching involved the temple.

Jesus and the Temple

EVENT	SCRIPTURE
As an infant, Jesus was circumcised and presented at the temple.	Luke 2:22–27, 39
Simeon and Anna, stationed in the temple, identified the infant Jesus as the promised Messiah.	Luke 2:25–38
At the age of 12, Jesus went with his family to the temple for Passover.	Luke 2:41–49
After his baptism in the Jordan, one of the Devil's temptations of Jesus centered on the temple.	Matthew 4:5; Luke 4:9
Jesus and his disciples went regularly to Jerusalem and to the temple.	Matthew 24:1–2; Mark 11:11; 13:1–2; Luke 21:5
Jesus often taught at the temple.	Mark 12:35; Luke 22:52–53; 23:5; John 8:20
Jesus healed people who came to the temple to worship.	Matthew 12:4–5; 21:14–15
The subject of Jesus' teaching often related to the temple.	Matthew 12:3–8; 23:16–22, 37–39; 24:2–31; Mark 13:2–27; Luke 18:10; 21:6–36
During Jesus' last week, he was found daily in the temple precincts.	Matthew 26:55; Luke 19:28–23:56, especially 20:1; 21:37–38
Jesus' referred to the temple as "my father's house."	Luke 2:49; John 2:16
Jesus confronted the Jewish officials and moneychangers at the entrance to the temple.	Matthew 12:12; Mark 11:15–16; John 2:15
At his Jewish trial, Jesus was falsely accused of planning to destroy the temple.	Matthew 26:61; 27:40; Mark 14:58
At the moment of Jesus' death on the cross, the veil within the temple was torn from top to bottom.	Mark 15:38
After his resurrection, Jesus spoke concerning Israel's future restoration (which would include the temple) and commanded his disciples to wait in Jerusalem for the promise of the Holy Spirit.	Acts 1:6–8

JESUS' LAST WEEK

Sunday

The Triumphal Entry

Jesus entered Jerusalem on a donkey and was greeted by crowds waving palm branches and shouting "Hosanna!" (which means "save us now," from Psalm 118:25). These crowds probably included many pilgrims who had come up to Jerusalem for the annual Passover celebration.

Matthew 21:1–11; Mark 11:1–11; Luke 19:28–44; John 12:12–19

Monday

Cleansing the Temple

In the Royal Stoa at the temple, Jesus confronted the moneychangers and drove them out saying, "It is written ... My house will be called a house of prayer, but you are making it a den of robbers."

Jesus then healed the blind and the lame at the temple. Children in the temple courts shouted to him, "Hosanna to the Son of David!"—enraging the chief priests and teachers of the law.

Matthew 21:10–17; Mark 11:15–18; Luke 19:45–48

Cleansing of the Temple. "On reaching Jerusalem, Jesus entered the temple courts and began driving out those who were buying and selling there. He overturned the tables of the money changers and the benches of those selling doves, and would not allow anyone to carry merchandise through the temple courts" (Mark 11:15–16). (Painting by Carl Bloch)

Tuesday

Teaching at the Temple

As Jesus was teaching in the temple courts, the chief priests and teachers of the law tried but failed to trap him in his own words. Jesus then taught the crowds a series of parables about the kingdom of God.

Jesus observed a poor widow placing what few coins she had in the temple treasury in the Court of the Women. He upheld her act her as an example of true giving.

As Jesus and his disciples were leaving the temple, one of his disciples said to him, "Look, Teacher! What massive stones! What magnificent buildings!" Jesus responded by predicting the destruction of the temple: "Do you see all these great buildings? Not one stone here will be left on another; every one will be thrown down."

Matthew 21:23–24:2; Mark 11:27–13:2; Luke 20:1–21:6

Olivet Discourse

After leaving the temple, on the Mt. of Olives east of Jerusalem, Jesus' disciples asked him about the sign of his coming and the end of the age. Jesus revealed to his disciples the signs of the end times.

Matthew 24:3–25:46; Mark 13:3–13:37; Luke 21:7–36

Wednesday

This day in not mentioned in the Gospels.

Thursday

The Last Supper

On Passover in an upper room in Jerusalem, Jesus and his disciples shared a Passover meal together. Jesus gave new meaning to the meal by identifying the bread as his body which will be broken and the wine as his blood which will be shed for the forgiveness of sins. After the supper, Jesus went to the Garden of Gethsemane on the Mt. of Olives to pray. There he was betrayed by Judas who had received 30 pieces of silver from the chief priests for handing over Jesus to them.

Matthew 26:17–56; Mark 14:12–26; Luke 22:7–23; John 13:1–30

Friday

Crucifixion

Jesus was arrested and taken to the high priests, first to Annas and then to Caiaphas. The Sanhedrin (the highest Jewish tribunal) accused Jesus of blasphemy, saying that Jesus claimed that he could destroy and raise the temple in three days. When Judas saw that Jesus was condemned, he threw his "blood money" into the temple, and went away and hung himself, overwhelmed by guilt. The priests decided that the money could not be deposited into the temple treasury because it was considered the price of a life.

Christ Before Pilate. "The chief priests accused him of many things. So again Pilate asked him, 'Aren't you going to answer? See how many things they are accusing you of.' But Jesus still made no reply, and Pilate was amazed" (Mark 15:3–5). (Painting by Mihály Munkácsy)

Jesus was taken to the Roman governor Pilate who, according to custom, was in Jerusalem to keep order during Passover when Jerusalem was filled with Jewish pilgrims. Pilate, when learning that Jesus was from Galilee, sent Jesus to the ruler of Galilee, Herod Antipas, who was also in Jerusalem. Herod was at first intrigued to meet

Jesus, a miracle-worker he had heard about. But when Jesus refused to answer Herod's questions, Herod ridiculed and mocked him, and sent him back to Pilate.

Though Pilate found no fault with Jesus, the crowds demanded that Jesus be crucified. Jesus was crucified on the cross at the "place of the skull" just outside Jerusalem's city walls. Even while on the cross, Jesus' accusers walked by mocking him about his words of raising the temple in three days. Yet Jesus prayed, "Father, forgive them, for they do not know what they are doing." At the moment of Jesus' death, the outer veil of the Holy of Holies was torn in two from top to bottom.

Matthew 26:57–27:56; Mark 15:1–41; Luke 22:66–23:49; John 18:28–19:30

Christ Appears to Mary Magdalene. "Jesus said to her, 'Mary.' She turned toward him and cried out in Aramaic, 'Rabboni!' (which means 'Teacher'). Jesus said to her, 'Do not hold on to me, for I have not yet ascended to the Father. Go instead to my brothers and tell them, 'I am ascending to my Father and your Father, to my God and your God" (John 20:16–17). (Painting by Alexander Ivanov)

Friday Afternoon, Saturday, Sunday Morning

In the Tomb

Jesus' body was laid in a tomb on Friday just before the Sabbath, the day of rest. The chief priests and Pharisees persuaded Pilate to place soldiers to guard the tomb because they remembered Jesus' words that he would rise in three days.

Matthew 27:57–65; Mark 15:42–47; Luke 23:50–56; John 19:31–42

Resurrection

Early in the morning on Sunday, after the Sabbath, Jesus' followers went to the tomb only to find that he was not there—he had risen! Jesus appeared to Mary Magdalene, Peter, two men on the road to Emmaus, and eventually to all his disciples and many others as well. The apostle Paul wrote of this saying, "For what I received I passed on to you as of first importance: that Christ died for our sins according to the Scriptures, that he was buried, that he was raised on the third day according to the Scriptures, and that he appeared to Cephas [Peter], and then to the Twelve. After that, he appeared to more than five hundred of the brothers and sisters at the same time…" (1 Corinthians 15:3–6a).

Matthew 28:1–13; Mark 16:1–20; Luke 24:1–49; John 20:1–31

THE EARLY CHURCH

Immediately after the account of Jesus ascending into heaven, the closing words of the Gospel of Luke say that the disciples were "continually in the temple, praising God" (Luke 24:53). The Book of Acts says that the greater company of disciples was daily assembled in the temple precincts (Acts 2:46; 3:1; 5:21), and especially in the Stoa of Solomon (Acts 2:46; 5:12–16), which was apparently their preferred place of meeting (Acts 3:11). The fact that Jerusalem became the hub of early Jewish-Christianity shows the respect these early Christians held for the sanctity of the temple (Galatians 1:18–2:2).

The temple was not only central for the disciples and the early church, but also for the apostle Paul. When praising the historical advantages of the nation of Israel, he included in his list "the temple service" (Romans 9:4). Even though Paul was commissioned as the "Apostle to the Gentiles" (Romans 1:5; Galatians 2:7–9), his faithfulness as a Jew to the temple service appears frequently in the Book of Acts.

Paul and the Temple

EVENT	SCRIPTURE
Paul observed the feasts according to the temple calendar.	Acts 20:6
He made religious vows (a Nazirite vow).	Acts 18:18
He participated in ritual purification rites—in one case involving four other proselytes.	Acts 21:23–26; 24:18
He made payment of ceremonial expenses, which accounted as a *mitzvah*, "a legally obligated good deed."	Acts 21:24
He offered sacrifices at the temple.	Acts 21:26; 24:17
He prayed and worshiped at the temple.	Acts 22:17; 24:11
He had regard for the priesthood.	Acts 23:5
He paid the temple tax.	Acts 24:17
He sought to prove to the elders in the Jerusalem church that he was as devout as any Jew toward the temple; he assisted others in performing their temple obligations.	Acts 21:23–26
He insisted on regulating his life by the temple calendar (the feast days), even interrupting his own missionary work.	Acts 20:16; 1 Corinthians 16:8
When he was tried before the Jewish authorities, he defended himself by affirming his ceremonial purity in relation to the temple.	Acts 25:8; 28:17
When he uses the analogy of the temple in his letters, he does so on the basis of the temple's sanctity, relating it with the sanctification of the individual believer's body, and the collective body of believers.	1 Corinthians 3:16–17; 2 Corinthians 6:16–17; Ephesians 2:21–22

Destruction of the Second Temple

Throughout the life of Jesus, the temple was the center of nationalist demonstrations and the Roman authorities feared a large-scale uprising led by a messianic figure. In this heightened atmosphere of conflict, it is understandable how Jesus worried the Jewish leaders (John 11:48–50).

- Jesus disrupted the moneychangers in the temple precincts (John 2:14–16; Matthew 21:12–13; Mark 11:15–18; Luke 19:45–48).

- Jesus made messianic claims (Matthew 21:14–16; John 10:22–39).

- Jesus predicted the temple's destruction (Matt. 24:1–2; Mark 13:1–2; Luke 19:41–44; John 2:19–20).

This fearful attitude increased as Jewish nationalistic ambitions intensified after the time of Jesus:

AD 40: When the Roman emperor, Caligula, commanded his statue be placed and worshiped in the Jerusalem temple, the Judean king, Herod Agrippa I, appealed to him to rescind his order to prevent a major Jewish uprising.

AD 44: When Agrippa died the whole of the country was placed under direct Roman rule.

AD 53: The Roman procurator of Judea bribed Jews to murder High Priest Jonathan in the temple, leading to a succession of murders during feast days at the temple.[75]

The Triumph of Titus. Titus' victory procession after his destruction of Jerusalem. Note the temple menorah depicted in the background. (Painting by Alma Tadema)

AD 66: When the Roman governor confiscated 17 talents from the temple treasury, Jewish nationalists staged a revolt, seizing the temple, stopping the daily sacrifices in tribute of the Roman emperor, and capturing the stronghold of Masada. This led to the First Jewish Revolt that ended in the destruction of the temple in AD 70.

Relief on the Arch of Titus, Rome

The First Jewish Revolt (the Great War) was unique in the history of the region since the Jews were the only people in the ancient Near East to launch a revolution on such a scale against the Roman Empire. This conflict began and ended with the Jewish temple. In response to the uprising, Rome's leading commander Vespasian was dispatched with four legions totalling about 50,000 soldiers. By the summer of AD 70, Vespasian's Tenth Legion arrived in Jerusalem and placed the city under siege. Jerusalem was one of the largest cities in the ancient world and had a reputation as being impossible to overtake. Even though the Roman soldiers were weary, they intended to make an example out of this revolt. The Jewish militant factions (the Zealots and the Sicarii) intended to crush the Roman occupation of Israel and drive the Romans from the land.

Vespasian returned to Rome to assume his duties as emperor, giving his son Titus command of the Tenth Legion in charge of completing Jerusalem's submission. The Jews celebrated a last Passover with their temple and prepared for the Roman attack. It came days later with a catapult barrage that continued for two months until the Romans finally breached the walls. They set fire to the city, slaughtering every Jew in their wake.

The Jewish defenders held back the Roman assault from the Temple Mount for three weeks. Then, on the ninth of the Jewish month of Av (August), the Romans invaded the temple compound and set fire to it and slaughtered the priests. The Romans chopped down the trees in the area to form a huge bonfire around the temple. This caused the moisture in the temple's limestone blocks to expand and blow the stones apart, collapsing the temple in a single day. Josephus records that the Romans pillaged the temple treasury[76] and storehouses of ritual vessels. The temple lay completely in ruins, with much of its rubble pushed into the Kidron Valley on the eastern side over the remains of the eastern retaining wall.

The following year, Titus was given a victory procession through the Roman Forum, and the temple vessels were displayed, carried by some of the 700 Jewish slaves paraded before the Emperor Vespasian. The depiction of this event can be seen today in the remains of the Roman Forum etched in one of the reliefs inside the Arch of Titus' Triumph.

Destruction of the Temple in Jerusalem. This painting shows the climatic events of the ninth of Av, AD 70, when the Roman Tenth Legion stormed the Temple Mount and set fire to the temple. The focus is upon the Great Altar from where, as Josephus records, Jewish priests flung themselves into the fire in vain hope that God would, at this last moment, be moved to deliver the temple which they had believed was immune from destruction. Also in view (lower left) is the plunder of the temple treasures (note the menorah) carried off by the Roman soldiers, a scene later sculpted on the Arch of Titus' Triumph in the Roman Forum. (Painting by Francesco Hayez)

TIME LINE: SECOND TEMPLE (62 BC–AD 70)

33

(March 30–April 3), During Passover week, Jesus enters the Temple Mount, disrupts the moneychangers a second time, and predicts the destruction of the temple. Jesus is crucified at the "place of the skull" and rises from the dead three days later.

(May 24) On Pentecost (Shavuot) Peter preaches in the Court of the Gentiles and 3,000 converts are baptized (Acts 2). Peter heals a lame man at the Beautiful Gate, identified by some scholars as the Double Gate, leading from the Monumental Staircase through the Royal Stoa to the Court of the Gentiles (Acts 3:1–11).

40

Roman emperor Caligula fails in his attempt to defile the temple by setting up a statue of himself.

5 or 4

In the winter season, Jesus is dedicated in Herod's temple and recognized there as the Messiah by Simeon and Anna the prophetess (Luke 2:22–38).

66

First Jewish Revolt (Great War) begins.

20

Herod the Great begins work to totally rebuild and expand the dimensions of the second temple. Work continues on the temple until about AD 64 (Matthew 24:1; Mark 13:1; Luke 21:5; John 2:20).

BC

AD

A

56

Paul goes to the temple with men completing Nazirite vows and is wrongly accused of defiling the temple by taking a Gentile there (Acts 21:26–28).

9

(April 29) Jesus at age 12 makes a pilgrimage to the temple at Passover and remains there three days to talk with Jewish teachers (Luke 2:41–51).

70

Roman General Titus destroys the temple and carries off the temple treasures to Rome.

36

Herod the Great besieges Jerusalem and captures the Temple Mount.

c. 26–34

Saul (Paul) is educated as a Pharisee under Rabbi Gamaliel on the southern entrance steps to the temple (Acts 22:3; 26:4–5).

32

(Sept. 10–17) Jesus comes to the temple at the Feast of Tabernacles (Booths) (John 7:2, 10).

(Dec. 18) Jesus comes to the temple courts at the Feast of Dedication (Hanukkah) (John 10:22–23).

29

In the summer or autumn at the beginning of Jesus' ministry, he is tempted by Satan by being taken to the pinnacle of the temple (Matthew 4:5; Luke 4:9). Jesus drives moneychangers from the outer courts of temple (John 2:13–17, 20).

ARCHAEOLOGICAL DISCOVERIES

Although religious and political concerns have prevented excavation of the temple site, there have been extensive excavations at the foot of the Temple Mount's massive retaining walls and western and southern enclosure walls and gates. These archaeological digs have confirmed the historical testimonies of Josephus and the rabbinical writings about the temple and its destruction.

1. *MIQVA'OT* (RITUAL IMMERSION POOLS)

Jews coming to the temple were required to ritually immerse themselves before entering the sacred precincts. To meet this need for purification according to the Law of Moses (Leviticus 11:40; 12:2-6; 15:11), ritual immersion pools or baths (Hebrew *miqva'ot*) were installed around the outside of the Temple Mount. Dozens of these have been uncovered on both the western side of the Temple Mount and particularly the southern entrance to the Temple Mount. (See *Court of the Gentiles* on page 78.)

Small ritual immersion pool located on the south side of the Temple Mount. (Photo courtesy of Kim Walton)

2. THE WESTERN (OR WAILING) WALL

This is one of three existing sections of the vast retaining wall of Herod's temple that has remained intact since the time of the temple's destruction in AD 70. This remnant of wall on the western side of the Temple Mount has gained a special sanctity in Judaism because of its proximity to the site of the ancient Holy of Holies, from which Jewish tradition teaches the divine presence of God never departed. As such, it has been a focal point of prayer for Jews from around the world. Here during the annual commemoration of the temple's destruction known as *Tisha B'Av*, Jews have offered prayers in mourning for national redemption. This practice led to the wall being identified as the "Wailing Wall." Today only 62 feet (19 m) remains exposed above ground. Due to the archaeological work from 1968 to 1998 that gradually exposed the ancient underground street, visitors can now walk along 1,000 feet (305 m) of this wall through what is known as the Western Wall Tunnels.

Dome of the Rock

50 ft (16 m) original height

Entrance to Wilson's Arch

62 ft (19 m) exposed height

Entrances to Western Wall Tunnels

50 ft (16 m) below ground

Modern Western Wall Plaza

3. "BEN HACOHEN HAGADOL" SARCOPHAGUS

In 2008 a discovery was made north of Jerusalem of the lid of a stone sarcophagus (coffin) made of hard limestone and engraved with the words in Hebrew: *Ben HaCohen HaGadol* ("son of the high priest"). The lid had been plundered from a nearby Herodian estate where presumably the high priest had resided, and it was used in later Muslim construction that sat on top of houses from the second temple period. This sarcophagus may be identified with one of the high priests who officiated in the temple between the years AD 30–70 (such as Caiaphas, Theophilus Ben Hanan, Simon Ben Boethus, and Hanan Ben Hanan).

Inscription with the name of the son of the high priest

4. ROBINSON'S ARCH

Named after the American scholar Edward Robinson who identified it in 1838, remains were discovered of the monumental arch that supported an immense staircase on the southwestern side of the Temple Mount. This arch was primarily used by the priests to gain private access to the Royal Stoa from the main street that ran alongside the western retaining wall of the Temple Mount. A large assemblage of Herodian period pottery was discovered in the rubble beneath the arch, giving evidence that the area under the arch was part of the marketplace that lined the public street. (See *Robinson's Arch* on page 74.)

5. PLASTER FRAGMENTS

In the excavations in the Jewish Quarter after 1967, Israeli archaeologists discovered inscribed plaster fragments in a Herodian fill. On these were partial depictions of all three vessels within the Holy Place—the table of the bread of presence, the lampstand, and the altar of incense—as well as the stepping-stone used daily by the priests to reach the lampstand for trimming its wicks.

6. THE ANCIENT STREET LINED WITH SHOPS

The remains of shops lining the Herodian street on the southwestern side of the Temple Mount were revealed in the late 1990s. Archaeologists found scores of coins and other items that gave evidence of commerce. These shops sold sacrificial animals and exchanged coinage (the silver Tyrian shekel) for the temple rituals.

Street Shops at the Southern Western Wall

The remains of the walls that form these shops, which were constructed of dressed stone, were actually openings created by the difference in height between vaulted rooms (that served as the substructure for the street) and a paved plaza parallel to the southern side of the street. Therefore, a street ran above these openings and the spaces below were used as shops, rather than shops being constructed as separate structures. Shops (with their entrances facing south) were also located on the Southern Wall under the staircase that ran alongside this wall and butted into the side of the monumental staircase. It is likely that merchants from these shops had spread their wares up into the Double Gate entrance and were those encountered by Jesus in the "cleansing of the temple" accounts in the Gospels.

7. STONES ON THE TEMPLE MOUNT

In the 1990s when archaeologists uncovered the remains of the public thoroughfare and market alongside the Western Wall, they found hundreds of large shaped stones lying in piles on the ancient street. These were the very building stones of the upper wall that had been thrown down by the Roman soldiers in their assault on the temple on the ninth of the Hebrew month of Av in AD 70. Most of the stones weighed 2 to 4 tons each, but some were in excess of 15 tons, and the force of impact in some places had caved in the large flagstones that formed the street. The stones remain today as a vivid testimony of the temple's destruction as well as the existence of the temple itself. (See *Stones* on page 72.)

8. MONUMENTAL STAIRCASE

The remains of this grand staircase were uncovered near the Double and Triple Gates. The southern access to this staircase was uncovered deep in the Kidron Valley near the entrance to the second temple-period Pool of Siloam (a Byzantine-period pool was previously identified as this pool until excavations in 2004 uncovered the original lower pool). It is now apparent that this was the main public thoroughfare for worshipers coming to the temple from the pool and from other parts of the city. (See *Monumental Staircase* on page 77.)

9. "PLACE OF TRUMPETING"

In 1969, near Robinson's Arch, there was discovered an ashlar stone about 8 feet long that bore the inscription: "To the place of trumpeting to an[nounce]..." Although the rest of the inscription is missing, it is understood that it described the custom of alerting the Jewish population of the beginning and ending of the Sabbath, a holy day in which no work was to be done. This stone was once the cornerstone of a parapet located on the edge of the portico that ran along top of the wall. The inscription designated the place where the priest was to stand in order to blow the trumpet that signaled those in the marketplace and lower city to prepare for the Sabbath.

Replica of the trumpeting stone. The inscription is shown above in the rectangle. (Photo courtesy of Kim Walton)

The Place of Trumpeting. (Artist: Uwe Beer; Courtesy of Alexander Schick ©www.bibelausstellung.de)

The Modern Temple Mount and Future Temple

THE TEMPLE MOUNT *AFTER* THE TEMPLE

Early Roman and Byzantine Period

After the Roman destruction of the temple in AD 70, the Jewish people continued to hold onto the hope for the restoration of Israel and the rebuilding of the temple. Initially, the Jewish population in Judea believed that the Roman emperor Hadrian had promised to rebuild the temple. However, in AD 130 Hadrian began building a Roman colony right on top of the ruins of the Jewish city! Two years later, a man named Shimon ben Kosiba led a Jewish Revolt against Rome. He was renamed Bar Kokhba, meaning "son of a star" from the messianic prophecy of Numbers 24:17. He successfully liberated Jerusalem in AD 132 and ruled as king in Jerusalem for the next three years—and he began rebuilding the temple.[77] It is unclear as to how much restoration of the temple site he was able to achieve, but from coins that he minted depicting the front of the temple and bearing the name of High Priest Elezar, it is believed that he at least rebuilt the altar of burnt offering and reinstituted the sacrificial system.

Bar Kokhba coin showing the facade of the temple.

Emperor Julian (reigned AD 355–363), known as Julian the Apostate because of his rejection of Christianity.

But the rebuilding effort was short lived. Hadrian recaptured Jerusalem in AD 135 and issued an edict banishing all Jews from Jerusalem on pain of death. Hadrian also destroyed whatever had been rebuilt on the Temple Mount. To make the destruction complete, he built a temple on the Mount to the Roman trinity: Juno, Jupiter, and Minerva. According to the fourth-century Christian scholar Jerome, Hadrian also placed a statue of himself directly over the site of the Holy of Holies.

Two centuries later, in AD 312, the Roman Emperor Constantine converted to Christianity and made Christianity the religion of the empire. However this changed when his nephew Julian succeeded him as emperor. Julian—who had been raised as a Christian but had embraced the former Roman religion—decided to promote a return to paganism.

In an effort to gain Jewish support against Christianity, Julian returned Jerusalem to its former status as a Jewish city and made plans to rebuild the temple. Julian lifted Hadrian's ban, allowing Jews to resettle in the holy city, while his construction engineer drew up plans for the temple. Christians prayed for the reconstruction to stop, and on May 27, 363, the day the work was to begin, an explosion at the construction site killed the workmen and stopped the work. According to historians of the period, an earthquake was responsible for igniting reservoirs of gases trapped below ground or volatile materials that were being used in the building. Christians, however, interpreted it as a sign of divine disfavor toward Julian's plan. Julian died shortly thereafter and the rebuilding project was abandoned.

For the next few centuries, the Temple Mount remained desolate. It is believed that the Christian inhabitants of Jerusalem turned the site into a garbage dump, piling tons of refuse particularly upon the spot where the ancient temple had stood. The gate on the western side that led to the dumping spot was called the Dung Gate, a name it still bears today. However, due to the Temple Mount Sifting Project, recent discoveries of coins, ornamental crucifixes, and fragments of columns found from Jerusalem's Byzantine era (AD 380–638) suggest that Christian worship activities also occurred on the Temple Mount.

A final effort to re-establish the temple came near the end of the Byzantine period. In the year 614, the Persians (Sasanian Parthians) invaded Jerusalem and massacred much of its Christian population. Favoring the Jews who had sided with them against the Christians, the Persians gave the Jews control over Jerusalem and plans were made to rebuild the temple. However, the Persians were unable to ignore the Christian majority in the land and Jerusalem was soon returned to Byzantine Christian control, a status secured for the rest of the country by the Emperor Heraclius in AD 629.

Islamic Period and the Dome of the Rock

While Jerusalem was in a period of strife between Jews and Christians, a man named Muhammad was unifying the Arab tribes in the Arabian Peninsula under the banner of Islam. Shortly after Muhammad's death, one of his successors, the Umayyad Caliph Omar, led his army of Muslim nomadic warriors in the conquest of Jerusalem. With strategic areas around Jerusalem conquered by Muslims, the Byzantine Patriarch Sophronius reluctantly negotiated the city's surrender in AD 638. According to Islamic tradition, Omar requested Sophronius to show him the temple site. When Omar saw the garbage dump on the site, he was appalled that such desecration had taken place on a site so revered by figures mentioned in the Qur'an (such as Abraham, David, and Solomon). It is said that Omar ordered the site to be cleared of garbage, performing an unprecedented act of removing a handful of the refuse himself. Beneath this pile of garbage lay the rock protrusion of Mt. Moriah, upon which he allegedly ordered the building of a "house of prayer."

However no actual structure was built at this site for nearly 60 years until AD 691 when Omar's son built a large wooden building known as the Dome of the Rock (Arabic *Qubbat al-Sakhra*). Omar had demonstrated his conquest of Christianity by praying inside the Christian basilica of Saint Mary built a century earlier by the Emperor Justinian and located at the southern end of the Temple Mount. This act obligated the church to be converted to a mosque. In AD 715 the Al-Aqsa Mosque was built in place of the church. Old photos of mosaics in the foundation of the mosque taken during a renovation in the early twentieth century reveal that it was once the site of the church.

To rival the local Christian architecture, the design of the Dome of the Rock was strikingly similar to Byzantine buildings. The Dome of the Rock was intended to be an architectural expression of the superiority of Islam. Over time the drum and dome inside the shrine were covered with ornate Qur'anic inscriptions stating—in contrast to Christian theology—that God is one and not three, and that Jesus was an apostle of God and not his son.

Entrance to the Temple Mount. The Dome of the Rock is shown in the background. In the mid-twentieth century, the lead roof was replaced with gold anodized aluminum, making it gold in appearance.

(Painting by Gustav Bauernfeind)

From the Crusades to the Modern Era

In the late eleventh century, Europe was faced with a growing threat. Muslim Turks had attacked strategic locations in eastern Europe and controlled much of the Middle East, including Jerusalem. They banned Christian pilgrimages to their sacred sites in Jerusalem and the Holy Land. In response, Pope Urban II in 1095 urged the warring kings of Europe to unite together to defeat the Turks and conquer the Holy Land in what was known as the Crusades.

In in 1099, the First Crusade succeeded in establishing Christian control of Jerusalem. The Dome of the Rock was turned into a place of Christian worship and renamed *Templum Domini*, meaning "the temple of the Lord," and the Al-Aqsa Mosque became initially a palace for the Crusader kings and later the headquarters for the Knights Templar. Muslims and Jews were permitted to visit the holy sites and pray in certain areas, but access was largely limited to Christians.

Richard the Lionheart on his way to Jerusalem in 1190 on the Third Crusade.

(Painting by James William Glass)

After almost a century of Christian rule, the Kurdish Muslim Sultan Saladin laid siege to Jerusalem and defeated the Crusaders in 1187. He expelled them from Jerusalem and tore down a large cross that had been placed on the *Templum Domini* and replaced it with an Islamic Crescent marking the beginning of the conversion of Christian property.

Shortly thereafter, the Third Crusade was launched to regain Jerusalem and was led by Richard the Lionheart. Though successful in defeating Saladin in several key battles, Richard did not ultimately capture Jerusalem. This Crusade ended with a truce allowing Jerusalem to remain under Muslim control, with the provision that Christian pilgrims be allowed to travel to the Holy Land, though not to the Temple Mount. Richard's decision not to attack Jerusalem eventually led to the Fourth Crusade six years later to recapture Jerusalem, but this Crusade also failed, not even making it to Jerusalem. During this period, Jews were allowed access to an exposed outer remnant of the temple compound's retaining wall known as the Western Wall. They also found access to a secret passageway beneath this area for prayer that was closer to the place of the Holy of Holies.

In 1516 the Ottoman Turks assumed control of Jerusalem. Four years later, the Ottoman Turk Suleiman, known as "Suleiman the Magnificent," became Caliph. He rebuilt the walls of Jerusalem which had suffered years of assault and dismantling during the Crusades. He made improvements to the Al-Aqsa Mosque and to the Dome of the Rock. Restrictions of non-Muslim access to the Temple Mount were strengthened under Ottoman rule. Several court cases from this period record the punishment of Jews who violated these boundaries. The Ottoman Empire remained in control of Jerusalem for the next 400 years, up to the end of World War I in the early twentieth century.

MUHAMMAD'S "DISTANT SHRINE"

Over the centuries Islam has come to claim the Temple Mount—which they refer to as *Al-Haram al-Sharif* ("Noble Sanctuary")—as one of their holiest sites. This is done on the basis of the account of Muhammad's Night Journey in the Qur'an.[78] In the Night Journey, which according to tradition occurred in approximately AD 620, the angel Gabriel takes Muhammad on a celestial horse to visit a "distant shrine."

Through the early Islamic period neither Jerusalem nor its Temple Mount were ever regarded as a place of Islamic pilgrimage, a fact not surprising since Jerusalem is not mentioned by name once in the Qur'an. However in the twelfth century, the Kurdish warlord Saladin mounted a large propaganda campaign claiming that the Dome of the Rock in Jerusalem was indeed the "distant shrine" to where Muhammad had flown in his Night Journey. The fact that there was also a mosque at the site called Al-Aqsa (meaning "distant" or "farthest") was used to make this claim certain and to justify an attack on the Christian crusaders who then controlled Jerusalem. Saladin's goal was to provoke a *jihadic* (holy war) fervor in the separate Muslim tribes to get them to unify in the siege of the city.

In this way, the Night Journey eventually came to be associated with Jerusalem. The large stone that lies in the center of the Dome of the Rock is believed by Muslims to be the spot where Muhammad ascended to heaven with Gabriel at the end of the Night Journey account. Every site connected with the *Al-Haram al-Sharif* (the Temple Mount) was deemed sacred Islamic property that had to be administered by an Islamic trust (*Waqf*). This includes, even today, the traditional Jewish site of prayer, the Western Wall, which Muslims call *Al-Buraq* wall after the tradition that Muhammad tied his celestial horse *Al-Buraq* at this spot.

Sixteenth-century painting of Muhammad's Night Journey. The prophet is depicted riding Al-Buraq, his celestial steed. In this painting Muhammad's face is veiled in keeping with Islamic tradition of forbidding depictions of the prophet.

Jerusalem Time Line

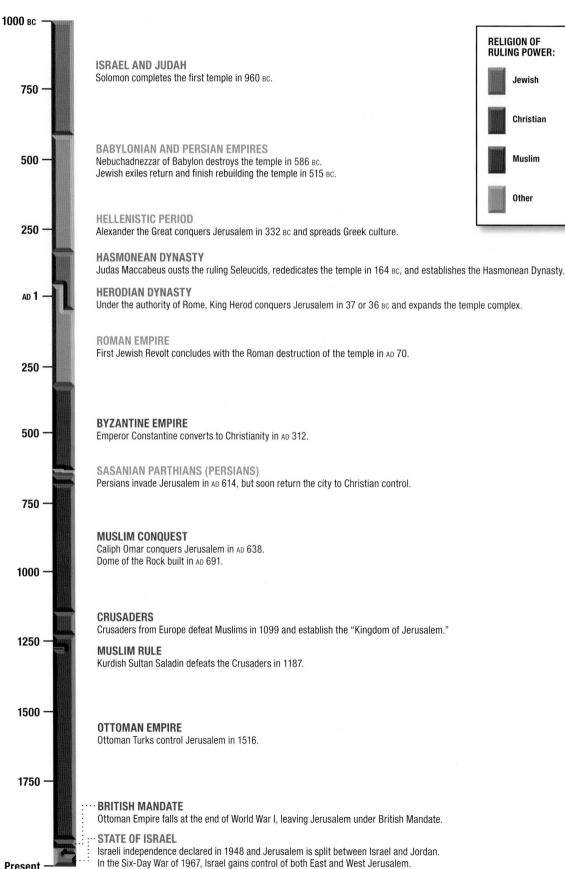

RELIGION OF RULING POWER:

Jewish

Christian

Muslim

Other

1000 BC

750

ISRAEL AND JUDAH
Solomon completes the first temple in 960 BC.

500

BABYLONIAN AND PERSIAN EMPIRES
Nebuchadnezzar of Babylon destroys the temple in 586 BC.
Jewish exiles return and finish rebuilding the temple in 515 BC.

250

HELLENISTIC PERIOD
Alexander the Great conquers Jerusalem in 332 BC and spreads Greek culture.

HASMONEAN DYNASTY
Judas Maccabeus ousts the ruling Seleucids, rededicates the temple in 164 BC, and establishes the Hasmonean Dynasty.

AD 1

HERODIAN DYNASTY
Under the authority of Rome, King Herod conquers Jerusalem in 37 or 36 BC and expands the temple complex.

ROMAN EMPIRE
First Jewish Revolt concludes with the Roman destruction of the temple in AD 70.

250

500

BYZANTINE EMPIRE
Emperor Constantine converts to Christianity in AD 312.

SASANIAN PARTHIANS (PERSIANS)
Persians invade Jerusalem in AD 614, but soon return the city to Christian control.

750

MUSLIM CONQUEST
Caliph Omar conquers Jerusalem in AD 638.
Dome of the Rock built in AD 691.

1000

CRUSADERS
Crusaders from Europe defeat Muslims in 1099 and establish the "Kingdom of Jerusalem."

1250

MUSLIM RULE
Kurdish Sultan Saladin defeats the Crusaders in 1187.

1500

OTTOMAN EMPIRE
Ottoman Turks control Jerusalem in 1516.

1750

BRITISH MANDATE
Ottoman Empire falls at the end of World War I, leaving Jerusalem under British Mandate.

STATE OF ISRAEL
Israeli independence declared in 1948 and Jerusalem is split between Israel and Jordan.
In the Six-Day War of 1967, Israel gains control of both East and West Jerusalem.

Present

Jews praying at the Western Wall. (Painting by Gustav Bauernfeind)

TIME LINE: THE TEMPLE MOUNT (AD 71–1034)

135

Hadrian puts down the revolt and rebuilds Jerusalem as a Roman city, *Aelia Capitolina*. He desecrates the Temple Mount by constructing a temple to Jupiter on the site, and bans Jews from Jerusalem.

130

Roman Emperor Hadrian plans to turn Jerusalem into a Greco-Roman city, *Aelia Capitolina*, and to build a temple to Jupiter on the Temple Mount.

363

Pagan emperor, Julian (the Apostate), allows Jews to attempt rebuilding of the temple to counter Byzantine Christianity, but an earthquake and Julian's death in battle shortly thereafter halts this attempt.

333

The Pilgrim of Bordeaux visits Jerusalem and records details of the temple site.

c. 400

Jerusalem Talmud completed by Palestinian rabbinic academies, preserving valuable information about the temple and its ritual.

313

Emperor Constantine issues the Edict of Milan, legalizing Christianity.

AD

c. 75–94

Jewish general, and later historian, Flavius Josephus (Joseph ben Matthias) writes his famous *Jewish War* and *Jewish Antiquities* which contain valuable eyewitness descriptions of the temple.

443

Hopes that Empress Eudocia would permit a rebuilding of the temple prompts letter calling for a Jewish return and messianic revival.

326

Constantine commissions commemorative structures to mark the supposed sites of Christ's death, entombment, and resurrection. His basilica was later incorporated into the Church of the Holy Sepulchre. His mother, Helena, founds basilicas at the Mount of Olives and Bethlehem, and according to later tradition, finds a piece of the "True Cross."

337–380

Visits to Jerusalem by Eusebius Bishop of Caesarea (337) and pilgrim nun Egeria (380) result in further accounts of the temple area.

565

A mosaic map is created in Madaba (today in Jordan) depicting walled Jerusalem and the Western Wall.

132

Hadrian's actions incite the Bar Kokhba rebellion, led by Simon ben Kosiba, who attempts to retake Jerusalem and rebuild the temple.

614

Persian conquest of Jerusalem, with the Jews as their allies, leads to Jewish hopes to regain Jerusalem from the Persians and to rebuild the temple.

617

Persia restores Jerusalem to the Christians.

715

The Muslim Caliph al-Walid completes the Al-Aqsa Mosque on the southern portion of Temple Mount. This is the Al-Aqsa *al-Qadimeh* ("eastward") underneath the present structure.

638

Muslims conquer Jerusalem and Caliph Omar Ibn al-Khattab is shown the Temple Mount and the site of the temple (Rock) by Jerusalem Patriarch Sophronios, and finds it covered in centuries of dung and debris.

1034

After earthquakes damage the Al-Aqsa Mosque, Fatimid Imam 'Ali al-Zahir rebuilds it.

AD

640

Caliph Omar Ibn al-Khattab cleans the Temple Mount and builds a mosque.

629

Emperor Heraclius conquers Persians and retakes Jerusalem.

691

Muslim Caliph Abd al-Malik Ibn-Marwan completes the Dome of the Rock on the Temple Mount nearly 70 years after Muhammad's *Hijrah* (flight from Mecca to Medina).

622

Muhammad's flight "hijrah" from Mecca to Medina. This is Year 1 of the Islamic calendar.

c. 921

Rabbi Aharon ben Meir (Gaon of Israel) writes that Jews, whose worship is usually limited to synagogue buildings, are permitted a yearly procession through Jerusalem to the Mt. of Olives.

c. 620

The Islamic prophet Muhammad is believed to have made his Night Journey from Mecca to Jerusalem, and to have ascended to the seventh heaven from the site of the holy rock (*al-Sakhra*).

TIME LINE: THE TEMPLE MOUNT (1035–1897)

1187

Saladin recaptures Jerusalem for Muslims and converts *Templum Domini* and Al-Aqsa to mosques.

1193

Al-Malik al-Afdal, son of Saladin founds the Mosque of Omar south of the Holy Sepulchre.

1099

Crusaders capture Jerusalem and transform Muslim Dome of the Rock into a Christian church (*Templum Domini*, "the temple of the Lord"). In 1118, the Al-Aqsa Mosque becomes headquarters of the Order of the Knights Templar.

1215

Rabbi Menachem ben Peretz of Hebron writes that the Western Wall still exists and that Jews live near it.

1516

Jerusalem conquered by Ottoman Turks.

AD

1537–1542

Sultan Suleiman "the Magnificent" rebuilds the walls of Jerusalem, embellishes the Dome of the Rock and designates the Western Wall as the official place for Jewish worship.

1264

Mamlukes under Sultan Baybers capture Jerusalem and repair the Dome of the Rock.

1165

Jewish philosopher, Maimonides, visits Jerusalem and prays on the Temple Mount.

1322

Rabbi Estori Haparchi (of Florence) describes the Temple Mount in his work *Kaphtor Vaferach*.

1267

The Ramban (Nachmanides) moves to Jerusalem and establishes the Ramban Synagogue.

1855

First non-Muslims since the 1187 expulsion of the Crusaders are allowed to tour Dome of the Rock and the Temple Mount for a large fee.

1853–1856

Crimean War fought to resolve control of Ottoman Empire, including the guardianship of Jerusalem's holy places.

1897

Theodore Herzl holds the First Zionist Congress and establishes that Israel must be the Jewish homeland, sparking waves of *Aliyah* (immigration) to the land.

1662

The false Messiah Shabatai Zvi arrives in Jerusalem, producing hopes that the temple would be rebuilt.

1891

Report on clearance of Eastern Gate by Ottoman authorities.

1838

Edward Robinson discovers an arch in the outer Western Wall of the temple that belonged to the monumental staircase to the temple area.

1887

Baron Edmund de Rothschild attempts to purchase yards in front of the Western Wall for the development of a Jewish community.

1777

Venetian Jewish prayers at Western Wall for Arab pogroms in Jerusalem.

AD

1865

Charles Wilson discovers another arch a little further north of Robinson's Arch in the western wall of the temple.

1799

The French emperor Napoleon Bonaparte invades Palestine and announces that he would restore Jerusalem to the Jews, but is defeated at Acre (on the northern Mediterranean coast).

1866

Sir Moses Montefiore makes renovations at the Western Wall.

1873–1874

Claremont-Ganneau discovers a Greek inscription forbidding Gentile entrance to the temple courts.

1833

F. Catherwood gains access to the Temple Mount and prepares detailed maps of it and the surrounding area.

1831

Egyptians, under Muhammad Ali, conquer Jerusalem.

1867–1870

Sir Charles Warren, on behalf of the Palestine Exploration Fund, conducts the first archaeological excavations in the area of the Temple Mount.

THE TEMPLE MOUNT TODAY

Following World War I, the Ottoman Empire collapsed, leaving the British Empire in control of the Holy Land. Jerusalem came under British Mandate although the Temple Mount remained under Islamic jurisdiction and Jews were allowed limited access to the Western Wall. In 1948 the British Mandate ended, the State of Israel was declared, and war separated Jerusalem into a western section under Israeli control and an eastern section (containing the Temple Mount) under Jordanian control. This separation continued until the Six-Day War of 1967 in which Israel gained control of the eastern section of Jerusalem and reunited the city under Jewish sovereignty. However, the State of Israel returned jurisdiction for the administration of the religious sites

Dome of the Rock

on the Temple Mount to the Islamic Trust (*Waqf*). Today, Israel controls the Temple Mount and opens it to all tourists, and the Islamic Trust controls the religious sites—such as the Dome of the Rock and the Al-Aqsa Mosque—and limits access to these sites to Muslims only.

Islamic Denial of the Temple's Existence

Following the Six-Day War in 1967, Muslims lost control of Jerusalem and its Islamic holy sites to the Israelis. This land, held by Islam for 1,300 years, came under the jurisdiction of a non-Islamic entity. This loss of sacred

Interior of the Dome of the Rock

Muslim property was viewed as a crime against the Muslim world that needed to be avenged through the prescribed means of *jihad* (holy war). Even though Israel returned jurisdiction to the Islamic Trust, the Temple Mount still remained under the sovereignty of the independent State of Israel. Since then, there has been a demand for a return to full Islamic control, not only of the Temple Mount, but also of the city of Jerusalem. This has given rise to political organizations like the Palestine Liberation Organization (which became the Palestine National Authority).

The propaganda that accompanied the Palestinian *Intifada* ("uprising") beginning in 1987 included an official Islamic denial that a Jewish temple existed and that Jerusalem was ever a Jewish city. Even though Jewish archaeological remains have been uncovered all around the Temple Mount and throughout the city, those who deny the temple interpret the finds as "pre-Islamic," being either Roman or Christian, but not Jewish. They claim that interpreting these remains as Jewish is simply to justify occupation of Islamic holy sites and is part of a deliberate attempt by the State of Israel to destroy the Muslim holy places and rebuild the Jewish temple.

However, this denial of the Jewish temple is a recent phenomenon. In the English edition of a guidebook to the Temple Mount written by the Islamic authorities in Jerusalem entitled *A Brief Guide to Al-Haram Al-Sharif Jerusalem* published in 1924 (and unchanged in all later editions through the 1950s), the following declarations are made concerning the Haram ("holy site"):

A Brief Guide to Al-Haram Al-Sharif Jerusalem, 1935 edition

> "The site is one of the oldest in the world. Its sanctity dates from the earliest (perhaps from pre-historic) times. Its identity with the site of Solomon's Temple is beyond dispute. This, too, is the spot, according to the universal belief, on which 'David built there an altar unto the Lord, and offered burnt offerings and peace offerings'."[79]

> "In the west wall of the chamber [beneath the south-east corner of the Haram], a door opens into a staircase descending to Solomon's Stables. This is a vast subterranean chamber…. It dates probably as far back as the construction of Solomon's Temple. According to Josephus, it was in existence and was used as a place of refuge by the Jews at the time of the conquest of Jerusalem by Titus in the year 70 A.D."[80]

Even though the location of Hadrian's temple is still debated, the guidebook goes on to state that the late Greco-Roman marble columns inside the Dome of the Rock were taken from Hadrian's temple of Jupiter.[81] This statement affirms that the Roman emperor—who ended the Second Jewish Revolt and punished the Jewish people by renaming Jerusalem and plowing the Temple Mount with salt—had indeed built a pagan temple, which history records was on the site of the Jewish temple. This official Muslim publication reveals that the Haram was clearly understood to have been the site of a Byzantine Christian Church honoring Jesus' infancy (at the temple). It states: "the two rows of massive columns with capitals inside the Al-Aqsa Mosque were taken from Justinian's basilica[82]… (probably on the present site of al-Aqsa)[83] … under the Haram is a chamber with a niche believed in early times to have been the *Cradle of Christ*."[84]

Interior of the Al-Aqsa Mosque. The white marble columns are believed to be from the sixth-century basilica built by Emperor Justinian at this site. The basilica had been built to honor Jesus' infancy at the Jewish temple.

This document provides evidence to show that despite the present public denial of the historicity of the Haram as the Jewish Temple Mount, Islam did not hold this opinion for most of its existence.

The Temple Mount Gates

There are 11 open gates that service the Temple Mount and 9 sealed gates. Of the 11 open gates, only one, the Moors Gate, is allowed to be used by non-Muslims. Most of the open gates have historical significance only within Islam, but the sealed gates all have some historical connection to the ancient Jewish Temple Mount.

THE OPEN GATES

- **Tribe's Gate** (Arabic *Bab al-Asbat),* located at the north-eastern corner of the Temple Mount.

- **Gate of Forgiveness** *(*Arabic *Bab al-Huttah*), located on the north side.

- **Dark Gate** (Arabic *Bab al-Atim*), located on the north side.

- **Ghawanima Gate** (Arabic *Bab al-Ghawanima*), located on the north-western corner.

- **Inspector's Gate** (Arabic *Bab al-Majlis*; *Bab al-Nazer*), also known as the Council Gate, located on the western side.

- **Iron Gate** (Arabic *Bab al-Hadid*), located on the western side, near the "Little Western Wall," a small extension within a residential area of the Western Wall.

Gate of Forgiveness (also called Gate of Remission) guarded by police officers.

- **Cotton Merchant's Gate** (Arabic *Bab al-Qattanin*), the closest of the open gates on the Western Wall to the temple site. During the nineteenth century this gate served as a place of prayer for Jews of Jerusalem. This gate is used at times for non-Muslim exit from the Temple Mount.

- **Ablution Gate** (Arabic *Bab al-Matarah),* located on the Western Wall.

- **Tranquility Gate** (Arabic *Bab al-Salam*), located on the western side.

- **Gate of the Chain** (Arabic *Bab al-Silsileh*), located on the western side. Some scholars have thought this gate to be the location of the second temple period Coponius Gate.

- **Moors Gate** (Arabic *Bab al-Magharbeh*), also known as the Mugrabi Gate or Moroccans' Gate, located on the western side. This gate was built over part of the second temple period gate known as Barclay's Gate. During the Islamic period, the external facade of Barclay's Gate was covered and the ground outside the Temple Mount was raised above the lintel of the gate. Around the time of Saladin (twelfth century), but perhaps earlier, this gate was built in the western wall above the level of the ancient Barclay's Gate. This is the only entrance to the Temple Mount permitted to non-Muslims.

Moors Gate, the only gate open to non-Muslims.

THE SEALED GATES

- **Golden Gate** (Arabic *Bab al-Zahabi*) is located near the northern end of the eastern wall of the Temple Mount. It may have been built in the sixth century AD as part of Justinian I's building program or by the first Muslims to repair the wall in the seventh century, the Umayyad Caliphs, but the present gate owes its form to the Ottoman Sultan Suleiman who sealed it in 1541. However, within the interior of the gate is a vaulted ceiling, arches, and columns that date to the Byzantine period, and some Herodian remains have been identified in pilasters on the outside of the inner section of the gate. Remains of a section of an

Golden Gate on the eastern side of the Temple Mount. The northern archway (right) is called the Gate of Repentance and the southern archway (left) is the Gate of Mercy.

Herodian column was observed by Charles Warren in the mid-nineteenth century, and an early double-arched structure was discovered in 1978 below ground, but it is uncertain whether it is the top of a gate or part of an arch supporting another structure. The outside face of the sixteenth century Golden Gate has a sealed double entrance that leads to the two vaulted halls. These two gates are known as the Gate of Mercy (Arabic *Bab al-Rahma*) and the Gate of Repentance (Arabic *Bab al-Taubah*).

- **Gate of the Funerals** is located on the eastern wall just south of the Golden Gate. Some rabbis have claimed that it is built over the site of the ancient Eastern (Shushan Gate) since it is almost directly opposite the Dome of the Rock which they consider the site of the temple.

- **Bridge Gate** is located toward the south end of the eastern wall. This gate formerly led to the Temple Mount by a flight of steps. The portal of the gate is visible from inside the Muslim Haram.

- **Horse Gate** is located on the eastern wall to the south of the Bridge Gate. This once was the entrance into the underground areas of Solomon's Stables (part of the passageway from the Triple Gate) from the east side. Solomon's Stables today is the site of the underground Al-Marwani Mosque.

- **Single Gate** is located along the southern wall. It once led to the area of the Temple Mount known as Solomon's Stables from the south side.

- **Double Gate and Triple Gate (Huldah Gates)** (Arabic *Bab al-Thulathe*) are located in the southern wall. They are now sealed, being bricked-up in the Islamic period. The Double Gate can only partially be seen, having a visible part of the Herodian lintel, but not in its original position. When the temple stood, the Double Gate was used by the public, while the Triple Gate was used by the priests for access to the Temple Mount and for storage. Although the ancient Huldah Gates were located inside the Temple Mount, the two sets of outer gates that led to them, the Double and Triple Gates, are sometimes referred to as the Huldah Gates.

- **Royal Gate,** located on the southwestern end of the western wall. Its name is a reminder of the Royal Stoa that was at this location.

- **Barclay's Gate** is located in the Western Wall under the left side of the Moors (Mugrabi) Gate. Part of the doorposts and lintel of the Herodian gate is visible from the within the women's prayer area. This gate received its name from James Barclay, the American Consul in Jerusalem in the mid-nineteenth century who discovered it from within the Temple Mount. In the Islamic period, the gate was dedicated to Muhammad's celestial horse Al-Buraq, and the gate was blocked with stones at the end of the tenth

Barclay's Gate. The large square stone shown here is part of the lintel of Barclay's Gate. A lintel is a horizontal support across the top of a gateway. (Baker Photo Archive)

century. The interior gate room is used as a seminary for Islamic students. Some scholars have identified this gate as the Coponius Gate from the second temple period.

- **Warren's Gate**, located about 120 feet (40 m) north of Wilson's Arch and inside the lower preserved portion of the Western Wall (underground access today is through the Western Wall tunnel). This gate was one of the four gates mentioned by Josephus that were entrances from the western retaining wall. It received its name from the nineteenth-century British explorer Charles Warren whose team first discovered it, but its location was lost and only rediscovered in the early 1980s. The arch of the lintel of this gate is Islamic, but its gatepost as well as the interior is all Herodian. This was the entrance nearest to the Court of the Priests and the Temple Court and therefore probably served the priests in bringing wood, sacrifices, and other materials to the temple. This gate was opened shortly after it was rediscovered by Jewish rabbis who were searching for the ark of the covenant, but because the gate was near the underground area beneath the Dome of the Rock, Muslim riots forced the Israeli government to close its access.

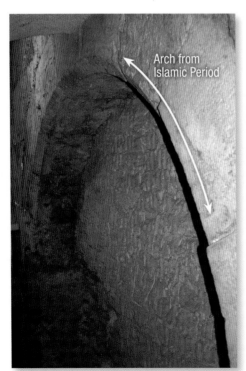

Arch from Islamic Period

Sealed Warren's Gate

Herodian Gatepost

Upper arch portion of Warren's Gate.

(Baker Photo Archive)

Lower portion of Warren's Gate

Plan of the Temple Mount Today

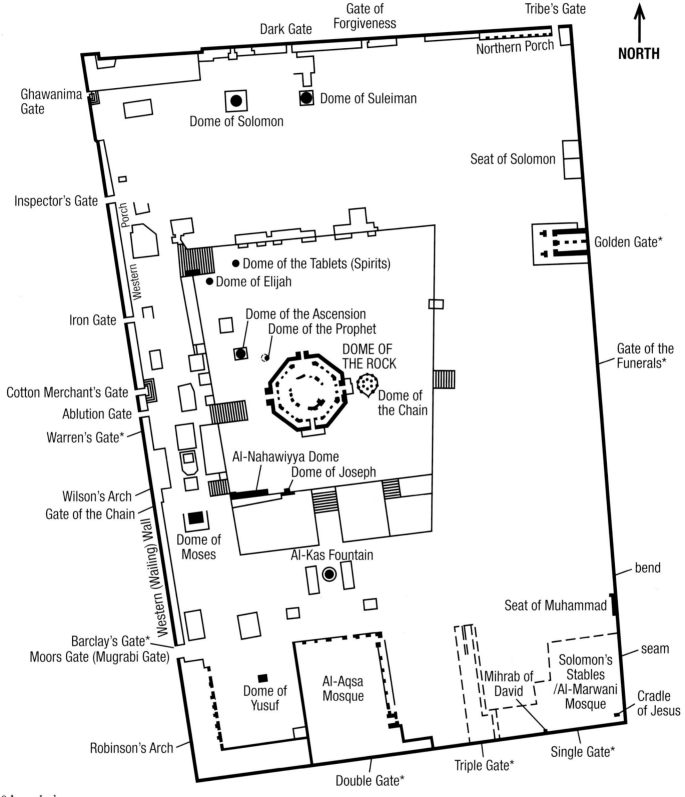

Gate of
Dark Gate   Forgiveness   Tribe's Gate

Northern Porch

NORTH

Ghawanima
Gate

Dome of Suleiman

Dome of Solomon

Seat of Solomon

Inspector's Gate

Western Porch

Dome of the Tablets (Spirits)
Dome of Elijah

Golden Gate*

Iron Gate

Dome of the Ascension
Dome of the Prophet

DOME OF
THE ROCK

Gate of the
Funerals*

Cotton Merchant's Gate
Ablution Gate

Dome of
the Chain

Warren's Gate*

Al-Nahawiyya Dome
Dome of Joseph

Wilson's Arch
Gate of the Chain

Dome of
Moses

Al-Kas Fountain

bend

Seat of Muhammad

Western (Wailing) Wall

seam

Barclay's Gate*
Moors Gate (Mugrabi Gate)

Mihrab of
David

Solomon's
Stables
/Al-Marwani
Mosque

Dome of
Yusuf

Al-Aqsa
Mosque

Cradle
of Jesus

Robinson's Arch

Triple Gate*

Single Gate*

Double Gate*

*A sealed gate

The Tranquility Gate is located on the western side. The Bridge Gate, Horse Gate, and Royal Gate are ancient gates whose location is uncertain.

Old City of Jerusalem Today

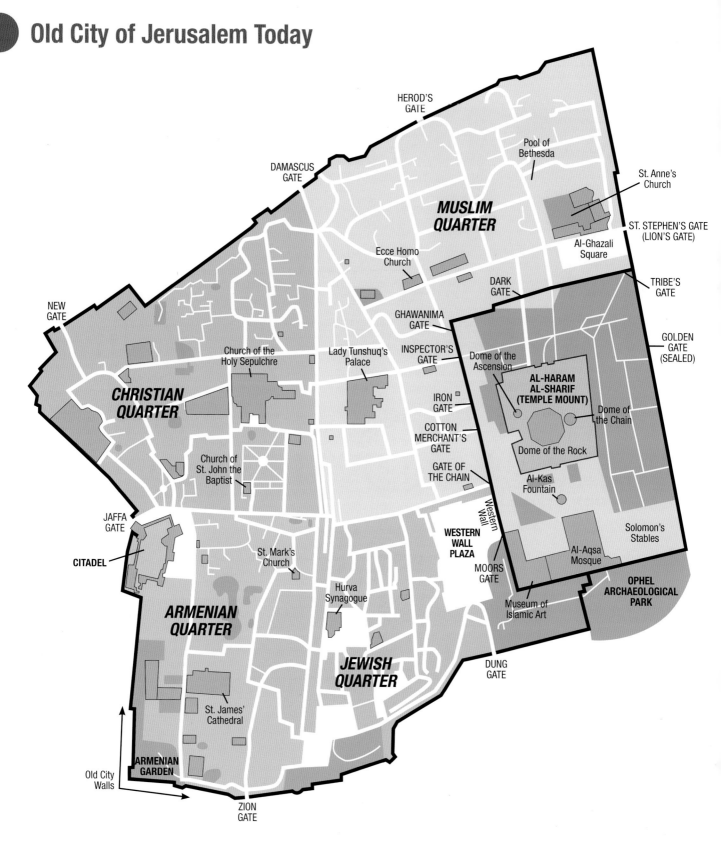

The Old City of Jerusalem is located in East Jerusalem. Ottoman Suleiman the Magnificent built the existing Old City walls in the sixteenth century. The State of Israel captured East Jerusalem (including the Old City) in the Six-Day War of 1967, unifying all of Jerusalem. The Old City is separated into four neighborhoods: Christian, Armenian, Muslim, and Jewish. (Armenians settled in Jerusalem in the fourth century.)

Locating the Site of the Temple

Ever since the Roman destruction of the second temple in AD 70, Orthodox Jews have prayed three times daily the words: "May it be Thy will that the temple be speedily rebuilt in our own time." With the return of the Temple Mount to Jewish control in 1967, many Jews believed it was a sign that the time was near. Some rabbis made plans to locate the site of the ancient temple and design a new temple.

Orthodox Jews have different opinions about when and how the third temple should be built.

- One school of thought believes that the temple cannot be rebuilt in a secular state, but will descend in fire from heaven completely constructed after a religious government is established with the coming of the Messiah and the Age of Redemption.

- A second school of thought holds that the Torah (particularly in Exodus 25:8) obligates the Jewish people to rebuild the temple whenever it becomes possible to do so.

In order to build the temple, the exact location of the former two temples must be correctly identified, because the space itself has remained sacred for Judaism.

Orthodox Jewish man prays at the Western Wall.
(©Mikhail Levit/Shutterstock.com)

The question of entering the Temple Mount also presents issues regarding ritual purity. Since a Jew cannot enter the place where the Temple previously stood in a state of defilement, the entire Temple Mount is considered off limits for many groups of Orthodox and ultra-Orthodox Jews. This defilement will continue, according to these groups, until the ceremony of the red heifer can be performed. Thus several attempts have been made to locate this heifer so that the necessary ritual purification can take place. Until that time, the risk of unknowingly entering a sacred space makes the entire Temple Mount off-limits. (See *Red Heifer* on page 75.)

The issue of rebuilding the temple has been at the forefront of the Middle East conflict. Many violent riots have taken place on and around the Temple Mount and spread throughout the country. Despite repeated attempts by Israelis and Palestinians to negotiate terms for the site, all efforts have failed and rigid demands have further polarized both parties. The Temple Mount remains the most volatile acreage on earth.

A man waves the Palestinian flag while thousands of activists march in Jerusalem for Palestinian independence and control of East Jerusalem (July 15, 2011).
(©Ryan Rodrick Beiler/Shutterstock.com)

While other parts of ancient Jerusalem have been buried under many layers of debris and buildings, the Temple Mount platform has been preserved down through the centuries. But where exactly on the present 35-acre Temple Mount stood the temple itself?

The large rock inside the Dome of the Rock. (Photo by Paul Streber)

The political reality is that the Islamic authorities forbid any access to the site for archaeological investigation and confirmation. Nevertheless, enough evidence has been gathered to come to a reliable idea of the location of the temple based on: (1) survey reports from nineteenth-century British explorers; (2) Israeli excavations below the Temple Mount since 1967; (3) occasional penetrations on the Temple Mount by the Islamic authorities for repairs; and (4) the recovery of archaeological debris from the Islamic construction of a mosque in the area of Solomon's Stables.

There are three main theories about the exact location of the temple. One theory put forth by Tel-Aviv architect Tuvia Sagiv, says that the temple was situated at the southwestern corner of the platform near where the Al-Aqsa Mosque is today. He also suggests from surveys of this southern area based on ground-penetrating radar probes and infrared thermographic scans, that traces of underground structures indicate the presence of vaults, such as would be expected beneath the temple.

A second theory is from Hebrew University physicist Asher Kaufmann who concludes that the temple was built on the northwestern corner of the platform about 330 feet (100 m) from the Muslim Dome of the Rock. He believes that bedrock identifiable within a small cupola at this site was the Foundation Stone within the Holy of Holies.

A third theory says that the temple stood exactly where the Dome of the Rock is today. Early research by Benjamin Mazar, the Israeli archaeologist who directed the excavations at the western and southern walls of the Temple Mount, and particularly Leen Ritmeyer who served as chief architect for the excavations, concluded that the original 500-cubit-square Temple Mount from the biblical period could be located from clues in the eastern wall of the Temple Mount that reveal pre-Herodian and Herodian additions, and existing remains on the Temple Mount. It was also possible to determine the site of the temple from a study of the arrangement of the temple's courts, which according to Ritmeyer could only be in the central part of the platform. (See Ritmeyer's *Dome of the Rock and Herod's Temple Comparison* on page 125.)

Ornamented walkways inside the Dome of the Rock. (Photo by Paul Streber)

Each of these theories place the temple either in the south, north, or central portion of the Temple Mount platform, but the exact location will only be finally proved once archaeological excavation can take place on the Temple Mount.

Herod's Temple & Dome of the Rock Comparison

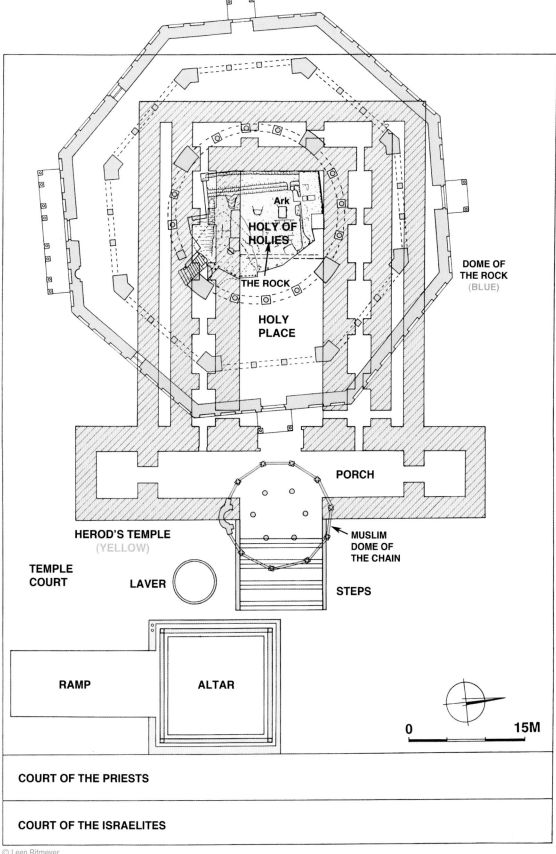

Ark

HOLY OF HOLIES

THE ROCK

HOLY PLACE

DOME OF THE ROCK (BLUE)

PORCH

HEROD'S TEMPLE (YELLOW)

TEMPLE COURT

LAVER

← MUSLIM DOME OF THE CHAIN

STEPS

RAMP

ALTAR

0   15M

COURT OF THE PRIESTS

COURT OF THE ISRAELITES

© Leen Ritmeyer

Cross Section of the Dome of the Rock

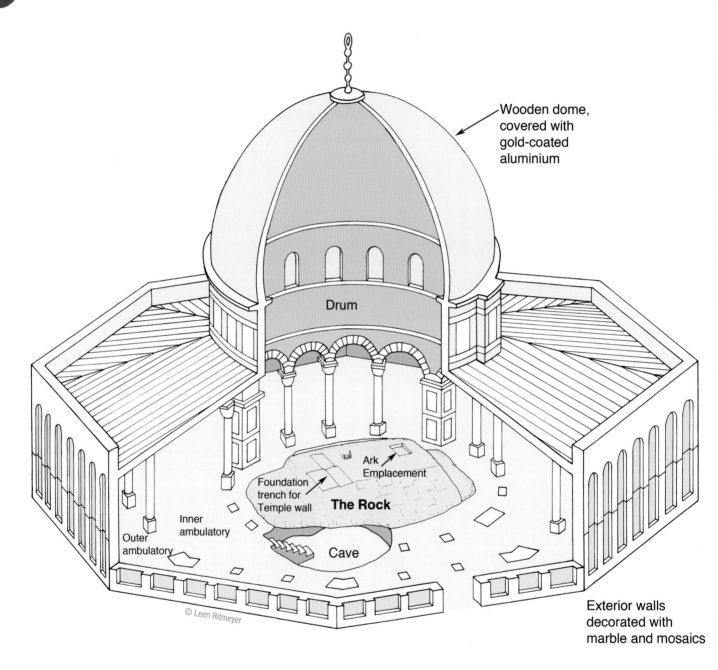

Wooden dome, covered with gold-coated aluminium

Drum

Ark Emplacement

Foundation trench for Temple wall

The Rock

Inner ambulatory

Outer ambulatory

Cave

© Leen Ritmeyer

Exterior walls decorated with marble and mosaics

This illustration by Leen Ritmeyer shows how the foundation trench for the temple walls is still discernable in the large rock inside the Dome of the Rock. In order to lay rectangular stones on the rock, flat areas needed to be created so that the stones would stand perfectly horizontal. Even though the stones have disappeared, these flat areas (foundation trenches) can still be detected.

This rock, according to Jewish tradition, is the place from which God created the world, and according to the Bible, the place where Abraham brought his son Isaac to offer him as a burnt offering on Mt. Moriah. In the first temple period, the ark of the covenant sat within the Holy of Holies on top of this rock, the proposed location indicated in the drawing as a rectangular indentation in which the bottom of the ark was set. The ark was placed in this indentation in order to prevent the ark from shifting when the high priest used its poles to direct his approach to the mercy seat of the ark.

View of the Temple Mount from the Southwest

NORTH

© Todd Bolen/BiblePlaces.com

1. Kidron Valley

2. Golden Gate (sealed)

3. Dome of the Chain

4. Dome of the Rock

5. Solomon's Stables/Al-Marwani Mosque (underground)

6. Repaired bulge in the wall*

7. Herodian Monumental Staircase

8. Al-Aqsa Mosque

9. Remains of Robinson's Arch

10. Old City Walls

11. Moors Gate (the only gate open to non-Muslims)

12. Western Wall

13. Entrances to the Western Wall Tunnels

14. Western Wall Plaza

*A bulge was discovered in the southern retaining wall of the Temple Mount, threatening to collapse a large section of the wall. Some Israeli archaeologists claimed it was due to the excavation of a new mosque in the area of Solomon's Stables. Rainwater became diverted into spaces in the construction loosening stones in the wall. Other archaeologists said the bulge existed before work began and reflects the weakness in the centuries-old wall. The repair work is visible today as lighter and smoother patches near the upper corner of the southern wall and near the southern end of the eastern wall.

TIME LINE: THE MODERN PERIOD (1898–1987)

1917

Jerusalem is conquered by the British in
World War I; continual struggles and riots
between Arabs and Jews, particularly
over access and control of the Western
Wall of the Temple Mount.

1920

Mandate for Palestine conferred on
Britain, giving Britain administrative
control over Palestine.

1929

Jewish worshipers attacked by
a crowd at the Western Wall.

1938

Rebuilding of the
Al-Aqsa Mosque.

1921

Supreme Muslim Council in
Palestine established with
offices located on the Haram
al-Sharif (Temple Mount). They
begin a program of restoration
work on the Haram al-Sharif.

1948

British Mandate for Palestine comes to an end.
Israeli independence granted, but no access to
Western Wall or Temple Mount. Arab-Israeli war
between newly independent Israel and her Arab
neighbors. The conflict concludes with armistice
agreements that grant Israel approximately
three quarters of Mandate Palestine. Hashemite
Kingdom of Jordan controls Old City Jerusalem
(which includes the Temple Mount) and Jews
are forbidden access to the Western Wall of the
Temple Mount for the next 19 years.

1967

(June) Israel captures the Old City Jerusalem during the
Six-Day War, reunifying all of Jerusalem, making the Temple
Mount part of the Israeli State. Israeli Defense Minister
Moshe Dayan returns religious administration of the site to
the Islamic Waqf; Magharibah Quarter destroyed, creating a
plaza in front of the Wailing Wall.

Moors gate closed to Jewish visitors until negotiations take
place which open the gate, but forbid demonstrative prayer.
Military police stationed at the gate to prevent its closure.

(Aug. 15) Rabbi Goren leads Jewish prayer
services on the Temple Mount, but Dayan
enforces the ban on Jewish prayer at the site.

1961–1967

British archaeologist Dame Kathleen
Kenyon conducts excavation at
southwest corner of Temple Mount.

1956–1964

Continued repairs to Dome of the
Rock, including replacing the lead
roof with gold anodized aluminum.

1968

(Feb. 29) Israeli archaeologist Benjamin
Mazar of Hebrew University begins extensive
excavations south and southwest of the
Temple Mount uncovering the remains of the
Robinson's Arch and the original entrance to the
Temple Mount through the Huldah Gates.

1951

King Abdullah of Transjordan is
assassinated by Muslim extremists on the
Temple Mount in the Al-Aqsa Mosque.

AD

1976

(June 17) Moshe Dayan makes an agreement with Muslim authorities known as the "status quo," in which the Muslims would retain religious sovereignty over the Temple Mount, while the overall control would be in the hands of Israel.

(Nov. 10) United Nations Security Council issues a Consensus Statement warning Israel that any profanation of religious buildings and sites would be a threat to international peace and security.

1987

First Intifada by the Palestinians against the Israelis.

(Feb.) A Jewish non-profit organization, the Temple Institute, is founded to raise public awareness about the temple and eventually bringing about the rebuilding of the temple.

(Oct. 11) The Temple Mount Faithful attempt to enter the Temple Mount as on the previous year, and are attacked by a Muslim mob.

1975

A group of adherents to the nationalist Beitar movement enter the Temple Mount to pray, but are evacuated by the Israeli-Arab police. The court judge rules in favor of the Beitar members, however, on the basis of the 1967 ruling that members of every religion may pray peacefully in holy places.

1980

(Aug. 10) Ultra-right Jewish activist group, Gush Emunim ("Bloc of the Faithful") with 300 supporters, attempt to force entrance to the Temple Mount and are dispersed by police.

1986

(Oct.) Members of the Temple Mount Faithful are permitted to visit the Temple Mount under heavy police protection.

1981

(Aug. 28–Sept. 10) Workers of the Ministry of Religious Affairs trace a leaking cistern to discover one of the original entrances to the temple (Warren's Gate); Rabbi Shlomo Goren closes the dig due to Arab rioting; Islamic and Israeli authorities seal the entrance.

AD

1973

(Aug. 8) Knesset member Binyamin Halevi and Rabbi Louis Rabinowitz pray on Temple Mount in protest of the government ban.

1982

(April 11) Alan Goodman, an American immigrant in the Israeli army, opens fire on the Temple Mount "to liberate the spot holy to the Jews." Though ruled mentally unstable by the Israeli courts, and later sentenced to life imprisonment, the incident set off week-long Arab riots in Jerusalem, the West Bank, and Gaza, and drew international criticism against Israel.

1985

(Jan. 8) Several members of the Knesset, led by Geula Cohen, seek to hold a prayer service in the temple area. The incident provokes a riot and an altercation with Arabs on the Mount.

1979

(Mar. 25) Rumors that Meir Kahane and yeshiva (Jewish religious school) students would hold a prayer service on the Temple Mount provoke a general strike among West Bank Arabs; Israeli police disperse 2,000 Arab youths brandishing stones.

1983

(Mar. 10) Rabbi Israel Ariel and a group of more than 40 followers plan to pray on the Temple Mount, but in a police search, authorities recover weapons and diagrams of the Temple Mount from the group and make numerous arrests.

1984

Israel annuls Muslim Waqf ownership of the Western Wall and declares it to be state property.

The Israeli General Security Service uncovers the Jerusalem Underground, founded by Michael Livny, Yehoshua Ben-Shoshan and Yehuda Etzion, a group committing revenge attacks on Arabs.

1969

(April 15) A Jewish organization, the Temple Mount Faithful, file legal action to allow Jewish prayer services on the Temple Mount, but the Israeli State Attorney upholds the government prohibition of prayer on the basis of national security and political concerns.

(Aug. 23) Australian Christian cultist Dennis Rohan sets fire to the Al-Aqsa Mosque; Muslims accuse the Israeli government of deliberately setting the blaze in order to rebuild the temple.

TIME LINE: THE MODERN PERIOD (1988–PRESENT)

1991

(Oct. 31) At the Middle East Peace Conference in Madrid, Spain, Syrian Foreign Minister Farouk al-Shara proclaims that there will be no free access to the religious sites on the Temple Mount unless Israel returns all of East Jerusalem to the Arabs.

1996

(Sept. 26) Palestinian leader Yasser Arafat provokes a riot on the Temple Mount when the Israeli government opens an exit tunnel to the Hasmonean aqueduct at the end of the Western Wall Tunnel. The riot results in 58 deaths.

1988

Jordan's King Hussein officially announces that Jordan relinquishes its claim to the West Bank territories, except for its holy sites which include the Temple Mount.

1993

Jordan appoints Sulaiman Ja'abari as the Grand Mufti of Jerusalem.

AD

1994

(Spring) Following Sulaiman Ja'abari's death, Yasser Arafat appoints Sheik Ikrima Sabri as a counter to the authority of the established Jordanian Mufti on the Temple Mount.

1995

King Hussein commissions extensive repairs to the Dome of the Rock; completed in 1998.

(Mar.–Sept.) The Herodian-era street running at the foot of the Western Wall is uncovered by archaeologist Ronny Reich.

1990

(Oct. 8) Renewed efforts by the Temple Mount Faithful to lay a cornerstone for the third temple provoke a riot on the Temple Mount. At the Western Wall where more than 20,000 Jews are assembled for Sukkot, 3,000 Muslim Palestinian Arabs pelt the crowd with stones from above resulting in a conflict with Israeli police killing 17 Arabs rioters.

1989

(Oct. 16) Gershom Salomon and Yehoshua Cohen with members of the Temple Mount Faithful attempt to lay a cornerstone for the third temple at the entrance to the Temple Mount during Sukkot (Feast of Tabernacles). The Temple Mount Faithful continue to petition to celebrate traditional Jewish ceremonies on the Mount, but are rejected by civil authorities.

(Oct.) Israel's Ministry of Religious Affairs sponsors the First Conference on Temple Research at Shlomo (next to the Great Synagogue).

1997

The Islamic Waqf begins renovating "Solomon's Stables" (Al-Marwani Mosque) in the southeastern corner of the Temple Mount.

1999

(Aug. 9–11) The Waqf opens an ancient door at the southern wall of the Temple Mount in anticipation of Muslims constructing a new mosque inside the Hulda Gate/Solomon's Stables area. The Israeli government seals the door despite Muslim protests stating that the Waqf's act does not affect the status quo of the Temple Mount.

(Oct.) The Waqf defies the Israeli government and begins construction in the southeast corner of the Temple Mount of the new Al-Marwani Mosque, removing some 20,000 tons of archaeologically rich debris. The Committee for the Prevention of Destruction of Antiquities on the Temple Mount is formed in response.

2006

(Oct.) Waqf construction to replace faulty electrical cable on the Temple Mount cuts a long excavation trench beside the Dome of the Rock. This trench reveals pottery from the seventh to eighth centuries BC and a large portion of a wall. Archaeologists determine that the wall is from the first temple complex and was probably associated with the "House of Oil" that was within the Court of the Women. This provided the first archaeological evidence for the location of the first temple.

2000

(Sept. 28) Yassar Arafat declares the Second ("Al-Aqsa") Intifada after Israeli statesman Ariel Sharon's visit to the Temple Mount to inspect the area where reports have been made of the destruction of archaeological remains by the Waqf. He accuses Sharon and the Israeli government of trying to destroy the mosques on the Temple Mount in order to rebuild the temple.

AD

2004

Archaeologists Gabriel Barkay and Zachi Zweig begin the Temple Mount Sifting project to recover and examine tons of archaeologically-rich debris from the Temple Mount deposited in the Kidron Valley by Muslims during the construction of the Al-Marwani Mosque. They uncover more than 5,000 ancient coins from all periods of the Temple Mount, Jewish seals with Hebrew inscriptions, and floor tiles from the temple courts.

2000–2003

(Sept.–Sept.) The Temple Mount is closed to all non-Muslims. Even when the Israeli government forces a return of Jews and tourists to the site, the Al-Aqsa Mosque and The Dome of the Rock remain off-limits to non-Muslim visitation.

2010

(Sept.) Israeli archaeologist Dr. Eilat Mazar announces the discovery of a long section of wall in the Ophel that she believes was part of the first temple.

1998

(Sept. 15) The first *Annual Conference of Shocharey HaMikdash* is held at an international conference center in Jerusalem, with approximately 2,000 attending to demonstrate their plans to build the third temple.

(Dec. 2) The U.N. General Assembly passes a resolution declaring Israeli sovereignty over Jerusalem illegal.

THE FUTURE TEMPLE

The biblical prophets spoke of a temple and priesthood that some scholars believe will exist in the future. A blueprint for a future temple was found among the collection of the Dead Sea Scrolls. The New Testament book of Revelation refers to a future New Jerusalem that the apostle John saw descend from heaven to earth.

The Temple Ezekiel Saw

Ezekiel lived in the sixth century BC during the time that the first temple was destroyed by Babylon and in the years leading up to the Jews returning from exile. He was of priestly lineage, and while in exile in Babylon he received his prophetic calling to preach to the Jews living in exile.

The book of Ezekiel (chapters 40–48) records with great detail a vision given to the prophet. The vision includes a magnificent temple far beyond anything anyone had ever seen before. Bible scholars are divided about whether to interpret Ezekiel's temple vision in a symbolic or literal manner.

SYMBOLIC	LITERAL
The temple in these chapters was never actually built when the people returned from exile and therefore it was not ever intended to be built. This is why the builders of the second temple did not follow Ezekiel's plan for the temple upon their return to Jerusalem, because the Jewish audience understood that the vision was only to be interpreted symbolically. There are several ways to understand the purpose of the symbolism: • It was meant to preserve the memory of the first temple through an idealistic remembrance. • It was meant to offer hope and encouragement for rebuilding the second temple. • It illustrates a spiritual ideal, such as God's dwelling in holiness in the midst of his people, or a spiritual reality (either the church, heaven, the New Jerusalem, or the eternal state).	The returning exiles were quite familiar with Ezekiel's priestly language from the descriptions of the actual sanctuary and its service in the books of Exodus and Leviticus. Thus, they would have expected to see these instructions literally fulfilled. The vision should be interpreted literally because: • The first section of the book of Ezekiel concerns the literal destruction of the first temple, so the second section with the temple vision should also be understood as a literal reconstruction of the temple. • Like Ezekiel, God gave a vision plan for the tabernacle to Moses and the temple to David, and Moses and David went on to prepare the construction of a literal, physical sanctuary from the vision. • The description of the temple in Ezekiel is extremely detailed, just like the instructions for building the first temple.

The Prophet Ezekiel

"In visions of God he took me to the land of Israel and set me on a very high mountain, on whose south side were some buildings that looked like a city. He took me there, and I saw a man whose appearance was like bronze; he was standing in the gateway with a linen cord and a measuring rod in his hand. The man said to me, 'Son of man, look carefully and listen closely and pay attention to everything I am going to show you, for that is why you have been brought here. Tell the people of Israel everything you see.'"—Ezekiel 40:2–4

THE DESIGN

Ezekiel received 318 precise measurements of the temple.

The Temple Complex

- The prophet Ezekiel saw the outer court and measured all the features (Ezekiel 40:5–27).

- The outer dimensions of the square temple complex were 500 cubits or 850 feet (259 m) on each side (Ezekiel 42:15–20).

- The prophet was led into the inner court where he saw animal sacrifices offered in this temple (Ezekiel 40:28–47).

- The Temple Mount had 12 gates, three on each side, named after Jacob's (Israel's) 12 sons (Ezekiel 40:30–34). This tribal allotment put the temple at the center of the nation, similar to the arrangement of the tribes camped around the tabernacle in the wilderness of Sinai.

The Temple

- The shape of the temple court was square. The altar was directly in front of the temple (Ezekiel 40:47).

- At the entrance to the temple building were two pillars located on either side (Ezekiel 40:48–49).

- Ezekiel entered and measured the Holy Place, and then his angelic escort entered the Holy of Holies to take its measurements which were 20 cubits x 20 cubits (length and width) (35 ft; 10.67 m) (Ezekiel 41:1–4).

The Chambers

- The chambers of the outer court were three-storied buildings with the roof of each at a different level, like terraces with the upper balconies set back further than those beneath them (Ezekiel 42:1–12). These buildings were accessed by a walkway that ran the entire length of the chambers.

- The southern and northern chambers were rooms set apart ("holy") for the highest order of priests who served in the inner sanctuary and whose responsibilities included the eating of their prescribed portion of certain offerings. These rooms also served as a place of storage for the three most holy offerings: grain offering, sin offering, and guilt offering. They also stored the priestly garments which had to be put on and then removed and returned to the sacred chamber each time a priest completed his appointed time of service (Ezekiel 42:13–14; 44:19; 46:20).

THE ZADOKITE PRIESTHOOD

Zadokite priests were the descendants of Zadok, head of one of the Levitical families that was elevated to the position of the high priesthood at the time of Solomon (1 Kings 1:26-27). The line of Zadok was prophesied to one day assume this position when the high priest Eli was disciplined by God for his failure to discipline his unbelieving sons (1 Samuel 3:12–14). The Zadokites were faithful throughout their service in the first temple period despite Israel's national unfaithfulness (Ezekiel 44:15; 48:11). But they did not continue to function as priests in the second temple period after the Hasmonean dynasty took control of the priesthood. If Ezekiel's vision is taken literally, when the restoration comes with the building of the temple, the proper Zadokite priesthood will also be restored (Ezekiel 43:19; Jeremiah 33:18).

> "This is the place of my throne and the place for the soles of my feet. This is where I will live among the Israelites forever. The people of Israel will never again defile my holy name."
> —Ezekiel 43:7

THE RETURN OF THE SHEKINAH

The prophet was led to the eastern gate of the temple to witness the return of the *shekinah* (the "divine presence" or "glory of God") to the temple (Ezekiel 43:1–9). After the Jews returned to Jerusalem to rebuild the temple in the sixth century BC, the *shekinah* did not return to fill the Holy of Holies in the second temple as it had the first temple and the tabernacle (Exodus 40:34–35; 1 Kings 8:10–11). The departure of the *shekinah* had started with a movement from its place within the Holy of Holies to the inner court (Ezekiel 10:4), then from the inner court to eastern gate (Ezekiel 10:19), finally to disappear in the east over the Mt. of Olives (Ezekiel 11:22–23). The return of the *shekinah* in Ezekiel's vision is the reversal of this order. The path the *shekinah* followed to reenter the temple went through the eastern gate (Ezekiel 43:4; 44:2). To commemorate this fact, the eastern gate was sealed shut and never reopened (Ezekiel 44:2). The glory that returned to fill the temple covered the entire mountain so that the whole city became "the throne of the Lord," giving brightness by night and shade by day as well as protection from storm and rain (Isaiah 4:5–6; Jeremiah 3:17). Since the restored conditions of land and people prevent future desecration, the *shekinah* will never again have to depart from the temple (Ezekiel 43:7–9).

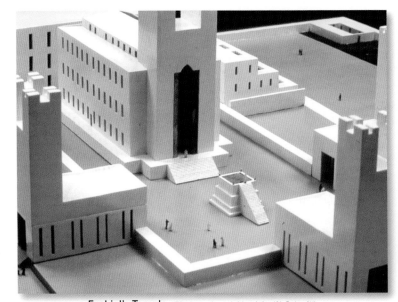

Ezekiel's Temple. (Photo and model by John W. Schmitt)

WATER FROM BENEATH THE THRONE

In Ezekiel 47:1–12 the prophet is escorted to the main entrance of the temple that faced east where he saw water flowing from the front part of the temple and running beside the threshold of the door and the right (south) side of the altar located directly in front of the temple (40:47). This implies that the water had come from God's presence within the temple from beneath the throne of the Messiah within the Holy of Holies.

Ezekiel was then led out of the temple area through the northern gate and around the outer eastern gate where he observed the water trickling from the south side of the eastern gate down south toward the city of Jerusalem and into the Kidron Valley. The river increased in size and strength as it descended to the Dead Sea. In the modern geography of the area Jerusalem is 2,000 feet (610 m) above sea level while the Dead Sea is 1,350 feet (411 m) below. However, in Ezekiel's vision the Temple Mount was even more elevated (Isaiah 2:2; Zechariah 14:10).

Ezekiel was next shown groves of trees growing on both sides of the river bank, certainly a startling sight for one accustomed to the normally arid and barren region. This change showed that the source of blessing is the Lord from whose house the waters have flowed. (See also Joel 3:18; Zechariah 14:8.)

THE GOLDEN GATE

Some Christians misunderstand this Golden Gate as being the eastern gate of Ezekiel's prophecy through which the *shekinah* will follow in order to reenter the temple (Ezekiel 43:1–4). The Golden Gate (or Gate of Mercy) located on the eastern wall was first closed by Muslims in 810, reopened by the Crusaders in 1102, then walled up again by the Saracens in 1187. It was opened again during reconstruction work done by the Ottoman Turkish Sultan Suleiman, but it was he who last closed it in 1541. We do not know for certain if the present-day Golden Gate is at the same place as the ancient Eastern Gate. However, the eastern gate of Ezekiel's prophecy is neither in the place of the present-day Golden Gate or ancient Eastern Gate, as Ezekiel's Temple Mount is elevated much higher (Isaiah 2:2; Zechariah 14:10). Some Christians have been taught that the presently blocked condition of the Golden Gate is a fulfillment of Ezekiel's prophecy. But it must be remembered that, if taken literally, Ezekiel's description of this gate and its closing concerns a future temple, not the Temple Mount that exists today.

The Temple Scroll

The Qumran community, known primarily for leaving us the Dead Sea Scrolls, was a Jewish sect established in the second century BC off the shore of the Dead Sea during the Hasmonean dynasty. This group was distressed over what they considered corrupted sacrifices. This is what had brought about the destruction of the first temple, and what they feared had doomed the second temple that existed in their time. This sect separated from the second temple to live in a desert retreat in order to maintain a proper ritual purity and to prepare for the coming of the Messiah.

Temple Scroll

Their quest for the ideal temple is most fully expressed in the *Temple Scroll*.[85] Scholars date this scroll to the second half of the second century BC (103–88 BC). The contents of the Temple Scroll include architectural plans for building the temple as well as detailed descriptions of the temple services and festivals—many not mentioned in the Bible or elsewhere.[86]

In this scroll, the Temple Mount is described as a square-shaped building surrounded by three concentric square courtyards, the outer court measuring a half-mile on each side. Jerusalem is described as being transformed into a temple city whose dimensions will encompass most of what was then the holy city. Another surprising element in the scroll is that the Holy of Holies contains the lost ark of the covenant as well the huge overshadowing cherubim, just as in the first temple.[87]

In AD 68, the Roman Tenth Legion invaded the Qumran settlement, set it on fire and then occupied it as a Roman fortress for the next ten years. Those in the Qumran community dispersed, with some fleeing north to Jerusalem and others south to Masada. Both of these groups eventually perished or were taken into Roman captivity when Jerusalem fell in AD 70, followed by Masada three years later. We only know about this community from its hidden scrolls not retrieved until the mid-twentieth century.

Cave 11 where the Temple Scroll was discovered. The last of the Dead Sea Scrolls were found in this cave. (Photo by Paul Streber)

The New Jerusalem

From the beginning when the Maker created humans in his image, he made them for a relationship with himself (Genesis 1:26–27). God revealed that he dwelt "in a high and holy place" (Isaiah 57:15) that was referred to as his heavenly throne (Psalm 11:4), his temple (Psalm 18:6), and the house of the Lord (Psalm 27:4). The garden of Eden revealed that God desired to dwell with his creation (Genesis 3:8). After the Fall, the temple that God commanded to be built on earth symbolized the means by which God could dwell with fallen humanity, an institution which made it possible for people to experience this relationship—but to a limited degree because of sin. By contrast, the New Jerusalem will be the fulfillment of the divine ideal in which God and redeemed people dwell together in an unlimited relationship.

OLD TESTAMENT	NEW TESTAMENT
• Abraham was "looking for the city which has foundations, whose architect and builder is God … a better country, that is a heavenly one" (Hebrews 11:10, 16). • God revealed the "heavenly city" to Moses (Exodus 25:9, 40) and David (1 Chronicles 28:11–19). • The divinely designated site of the temple was Jerusalem (Genesis 22:2, 14). • The earthly Jerusalem is described as God's "dwelling place" projected heavenward, forming the hope of an eternal city, the New Jerusalem where the relationship of God with his people will last forever (Isaiah 66:22).	• The apostle Paul speaks of "the Jerusalem above" in contrast to "the present Jerusalem" (Galatians 4:25–26). • The author of the book of Hebrews makes reference to the "heavenly Jerusalem" (Hebrews 12:22), also called "Mount Zion" and "the city of the living God" where there are myriads of angels, the general assembly of the first-born who are enrolled in heaven (the church), the spirits of righteous people made perfect (Old Testament believers), and God and Jesus (Hebrews 12:22–24). • In the book of Revelation, the apostle John sees a new heaven and earth, and a new Jerusalem coming down out of heaven from God (Revelation 21).

THE NEW JERUSALEM IN THE BOOK OF REVELATION

The New Jerusalem is a city "laid out as a square" with connecting planes of equal size that form a cube 1,500 miles (2,414 km). (This would be about the distance from London to Istanbul, or New York City to Denver.) Its gates are inscribed with the names of the 12 tribes of Israel and the foundation stones of its wall with the names of the 12 apostles (Revelation 21:12–14). Associating the 12 tribes with a certain type of precious stone goes back to the time of the first temple where the breastplate of the ephod worn by the high priest bore the names of each of the twelve tribes of Israel inscribed on a different type of stone. The streets are pure gold like transparent glass (Revelation 21:21). In Exodus 24 when God allows Moses and the elders of Israel to see him, their vision was of God's heavenly court where the streets were "a pavement of sapphire as clear as the sky" (verse 10).

John describes the New Jerusalem as "having the glory of God" (Revelation 21:11). The supernatural illumination of the city is the result of the presence of God and the reason why there can be no night there (Revelation 22:5). The original pattern of the garden of Eden is also present in the city, complete with a river of the water of life and the Tree of Life (Revelation 22:1–2).

THE TEMPLE OF THE NEW JERUSALEM

Throughout the judgment section of Revelation (chapters 6–19), John is taken to heaven and shown the heavenly response to the events transpiring on earth. For example, in Revelation 11:18–19 the heavenly temple is seen open with symbols of divine judgment proceeding out toward the earthly offenders. This prepared those enduring the conflict on earth for the revealing of the coming of Christ as well as for the New Jerusalem which comes "out of heaven from God" (Revelation 21:2, 10).

However, as John comes to the end of his description of the New Jerusalem he writes, "I did not see a temple in the city…" (Revelation 21:22). Such a statement would have been startling to those accustomed to viewing the temple as the place of the divine presence which will fill and illumine this city (21:23–24; 22:5). But John goes on to explain why he did not see a temple, "… because the Lord God Almighty and the Lamb are its temple" (21:22). The New Jerusalem is unique: It has no temple in the sense that it contains one, yet it has a temple in the sense that it is a part of one, that is, the heavenly temple. The cubic dimensions of the New Jerusalem are similar to those of the Holy of Holies within the earthly temples (1 Kings 6:19–20). Therefore, it appears that the New Jerusalem represents the Holy of Holies of the heavenly temple in which God in his glory is manifested. God is the temple of the New Jerusalem. The earthly temples were symbols of the presence of God with his people, but at the same time they were mere copies of the heavenly temple which is the presence of God. In the New Jerusalem, as in all of God's created order, he is all in all.

OUR FATHER'S HOUSE

The New Jerusalem has always existed in heaven and its descent to earth is still to come. Jesus promised to those who accept him that it is possible to go there upon death: "In my Father's house are many rooms … I go to prepare a place for you" (John 14:2). These "rooms" are not individual dwellings apart from the Lord, as if he lived on a hilltop and we all had mansions somewhere on his land. Rather, there is only one house—"the Father's house"—and all of the rooms are in it. But this is not some gigantic apartment complex; since the role of believers will be to "serve him day and night in his temple" (Revelation 7:15; 22:3), this means that "the Father's house" is "his temple."

In this temple, rather than one man serving as high priest for the people of God, all of God's people are high priests. Unlike the earthly high priest who could rarely enter the Holy of Holies, we will forever remain there. Our service is not once a year on the Day of Atonement, but will be day and night forever. The presence of God will not dwell within the Holy of Holies away from people, but God and the Lamb (Christ) will dwell among all of the redeemed. This is the great and heavenly hope of all who "seek his face" (Psalm 17:15; 27:8; 42:2; 105:4).

THE PRESENCE OF GOD

Revelation 21:3 says, "The tabernacle of God is among men, and he shall dwell among them, and they shall be his people, and God himself shall be among them" (NASB).

The word "tabernacle" (Hebrew *mishkan*, "dwelling place") refers to the idea that the divine presence (*shekinah*) is dwelling with humanity. The past prohibition, "you cannot see my face, for no one may see me and live" (Exodus 33:20; also John 1:18; 1 Timothy 1:17; 6:16) is clearly reversed in Revelation 22:4, for all those who are within the New Jerusalem will see God "face to face."

Notes

1. Donald W. Parry, ed., *Temples of the Ancient World: Ritual and Symbolism* (Salt Lake City: Deseret Book Company, 1994), 134.
2. Josephus, *Antiquities* 20.9.7; 221–22
3. *Middot* 2.1
4. The artist is grateful to the late Dr. Louis Goldberg who, with his engineering and theological background, assisted the artist in this reconstruction.
5. John Monson, "The New 'Ain Dara temple: Closest Solomonic Parallel," *Biblical Archaeology Review* 26:3 (May/June 2000)
6. *Antiquities* xi, 1.2
7. *Antiquities* 15,400; *War* 5.185
8. *Middot* 2:1
9. *Antiquities* 8.96; *War* 5.184–185
10. Ecclesiasticus 50:1–21
11. *Antiquities* 14.3.1–4.4; *War* 1.7.6
12. Tacitus, *Histories* 5.9.1
13. *Antiquities* xi. 392–339
14. 1 Maccabees 1:10–63; 2 Maccabees 5:1
15. *Temple Scroll* (11Q19)
16. 1 Maccabees 4
17. *Antiquities* 14.476
18. *Antiquities* 17.6.1–3; 151–63; War 1.33.2–4; 649–55
19. *Antiquities* 15.391
20. *Antiquities* 15.388–89
21. *Antiquities* 15.11.5–6; 420–21
22. *Antiquities* 20.219
23. *Antiquities* 8.97; 15.398, 400; 20.221; *War* 5.192
24. *Antiquities* 15.11.2; 389–90
25. *Antiquities* 15.412; *War* 5.207–226; *Middot* 4
26. *Antiquities* 15.413–414
27. *Antiquities* 15.11.5; 410
28. *Middot* 1:3
29. *Para* 3:6; *Šekalim* 4:2
30. Rabbi Chaim Richman, *The Mystery of the Red Heifer: Divine Promise of Purity* (Jerusalem: Rabbi Chaim Richman, 1997), 1.
31. *Apion* 2.8; 103–109
32. *Kelim* 1.8–9
33. *Antiquities* 15.11.3; 396
34. *Kelim* 1.8
35. *Middot* 2.5–6
36. Tacitus, *Histories* 5.8.1
37. *War* 5.5.2, 200; 6.5.2, 282; see *Antiquities* 19.6.1; 294
38. *Middot* 2.5
39. *Middot* 2.6
40. *Middot* 2.6
41. *War* 5.5.6; 225; *Middot* 3.1, 6; 5.2; *Tamid* 1.4
42. *Middot* 5.4
43. *Erubin* 10.14
44. *Shekalim* 6:1–2; *Yoma* 52a–54a
45. *Yoma* 3.10; *Tamid* 1.4; 3.8
46. *Middot* 3.2
47. *Middot* 3.5
48. *War* 5.5; 6.222
49. *War* 5.5.4; 207; *Middot* 4.7
50. *War* 5.5.6; 223–24; *Middot* 4.6
51. *War* 5.5.3; 206; *Middot* 3.6
52. Tacitus, *Histories* 5.5
53. *Antiquities* 15.394–395; *War* 5.210
54. *Middot* 4.3–4; *War* 5.220–221
55. *War* 5.208
56. *Middot* 4.1
57. *War* 5.211–214
58. *Shekalim* 8, 5; *Tamid* 29a, b.
59. Mishnah tractate *Tamid*; *War* 5.5.5; 217; Luke 1:5–25
60. *War* 7.148–50
61. *War* 5.5.4; 212–13; 5.5.5; 219
62. *Shekalim* 8.5
63. *Yoma* 5.1
64. *Vita Mos.* 2.101
65. *Shekalim* 4.4; *Middot* 4.1
66. Parshat *Acharei Mot*, p. 67a; Parashat *Emor*, p. 102a
67. *Yoma* 5:2
68. *War* 5.219
69. *Yoma* 5.2
70. *War* 5.5.5; 219; *Middot* 4.7
71. *Antiquities* 18.8.2–9; 261–309; *War* 2.10.1–5; 184–203
72. *Spec. Laws*, 1.141–44; 66–345; *Embassy* 156
73. 1 *Enoch* 89.73
74. *Tobit* 14.5; 1 *Enoch* 90.28–29
75. *Antiquities* 20.8
76. *Antiquities* 17:254–64; *War* 2.3.2–3; 45–50
77. Mishneh Torah 14 (*Sefer Shoftim*), *Melochim* 11:4
78. Sura 17
79. *A Brief Guide to Al-Haram Al-Sharif*, p. 4
80. *A Brief Guide*, 16
81. *A Brief Guide*, 10
82. *A Brief Guide*, 14
83. *A Brief Guide*, 1
84. *A Brief Guide*, 16
85. *Temple Scroll* (11Q19)
86. *Temple Scroll* (11Q19) 29:3–10
87. *Temple Scroll* (11Q19) 7:10–12

BIBLIOGRAPHY

The Biblical Engineer: How the Temple in Jerusalem was Built by Max Schwartz (N.J.: KTAV Publishing House, Inc., 2002)

Carta's Illustrated Encyclopedia of the Holy Temple in Jerusalem by Israel Ariel and Chaim Richman (Jerusalem: The Temple Institute and Carta, 2005)

The Complete Guide to the Temple Mount Excavations by Eilat Mazar (Jerusalem: The Old City Press, 2002)

The Desecration and Restoration of the Temple as an Eschatological Motif in the Tanach, Jewish Apocalyptic Literature, and the New Testament by Randall Price (Ann Arbor, MI: UMI, 1993)

Envisioning the Temple: Scrolls, Stones, and Symbols by Adolfo Roitman (Jerusalem: The Israel Museum, 2003)

The Holy Temple Revisited by Liebel Reznick (New Jersey: Jason Aronson, Inc., 1990)

In the Shadow of the Temple: The Discovery of Ancient Jerusalem by Meir Ben-Dov; Translated by Ina Friedman (New York: Harper & Row, 1985)

Jerusalem's Temple Mount: From Solomon to the Golden Dome by Hershel Shanks (Continuum International, 2007)

Josephus: The Complete Works by William Whiston (Thomas Nelson, 1998)

Messiah's Coming Temple: Ezekiel's Prophetic Vision of the Future Temple by John W. Schmitt and J. Carl Laney (Grand Rapids: Kregel Publications, 1997)

The Mountain of the Lord by Benjamin Mazar (New York: Doubleday & Co., 1975)

The Quest: Revealing the Temple Mount in Jerusalem by Leen Ritmeyer; Edited by Barbara Laurel Ball (Jerusalem: Carta Jerusalem & The Lamb Foundation, 2006)

Reconstructing Herod's Temple Mount in Jerusalem by Kathleen Ritmeyer and Leen Ritmeyer (BAR offprint. New York: Biblical Archaeology Society, 1991)

The Temple: Its Ministry and Services Updated Ed. by Alfred Edersheim (Hendrickson, 1994)

The Temple: Its Symbolism and Meaning Then and Now by Joshua Berman (New Jersey: Jason Aronson, Inc., 1995)

The Temple in Bible Prophecy: A Definitive Look at Its Past, Present, and Future by Randall Price (Eugene, OR: Harvest House Publishers, 2005)

"The Temple in the Book of Acts" by Randall Price in *A Bible Handbook to the Acts of the Apostles*. Edited by Mal Couch (Grand Rapids: Kregel Publications, 1999, pp. 109-118)

Temples and Temple Service in Ancient Israel by Menahem Haran (Oxford: Claredon Press, 1978)

Where Heaven and Earth Meet: Jerusalem's Sacred Esplanade by editors Oleg Grabar and Benjamin Z. Kedar (University of Texas Press, 2010)

WEBSITES

Bible Placcs blog (Todd Bolen) http://blog.bibleplaces.com
The Messiah in the Temple Foundation www.themessiahinthetemple.com
Ritmeyer Archaeological Design (Leen Ritmeyer) www.ritmeyer.com
The Temple Mount in Jerusalem www.templemount.org
World of the Bible Ministries (Randall Price) www.worldofthebible.com

The inclusion of a work does not necessarily mean endorsement of all its contents or of other works by the same author(s).

INDEX

Gilead 23
Gilgal 23
Golan 23
Golden Gate 75, 119, 121, 122, 127, 135
Goshen 23
Grain (Meal) Offering 43
Great Bitter Lake 23
Guilt Offering 43

H

Hadrian 106, 112, 117
Haggai 59, 60
Hanukkah. *See* Feast of Dedication
Hasmonean Dynasty 22, 62, 64, 66, 67, 70, 92, 110, 130, 134, 136
Hazeroth 23
Hazor 23
Heavenly Temple 1, 6, 138
Hebron 23
Hellenism 63, 66, 67, 92, 110
Herod Antipas 66, 95
Herod Archelaus 66, 67
Herod the Great 16, 22, 62, 66, 67, 70, 71, 73, 74, 76, 79, 84, 85, 88, 92, 100, 110, 122
Hezekiah 22, 51, 62
High Priest 4, 5, 7, 9, 14, 26, 30, 31, 40, 41, 46, 59, 60, 63, 64, 65, 67, 86, 87, 92, 102, 126, 134, 137, 138
Hijrah 113
Hiram 20, 24
Holy of Holies 5, 6, 9, 14, 15, 25, 27, 29, 30, 31, 46, 49, 51, 54, 64, 65, 70, 84, 86, 87, 96, 106, 108, 124, 126, 133, 134, 136, 138
Holy Place 7, 14, 25, 29, 30, 31, 40, 46, 51, 64, 65, 84, 86, 87, 102, 133
Holy Spirit 5, 15, 45, 46, 78, 80, 93
Horse Gate 119, 121
Huldah Gates 75, 77, 78, 119, 128
Huram-Abi 24

I

Inspector's Gate 118, 121, 122
Intifada 117, 129, 131
Iron Gate 118, 121, 122
Israel, State of 116, 117, 122

J

Jabal al Lawz 23
Jabesh-gilead 23

Jebusites 20, 21, 22
Jeremiah 48, 134
Jericho 23
Jeroboam 48
Jewish Revolt (Great War) 70, 98, 100, 106, 110, 117
Jezreel 23
Jihad 109, 116
Joppa 23
Jordan River 23
Josephus 16, 17, 58, 60, 65, 66, 70, 73, 78, 84, 86, 87, 99, 101, 112, 117, 120
Joshua the High Priest 60
Judah 48, 49, 50, 51, 60, 61, 110
Judas Iscariot 81, 95
Julian 106, 112
Justinian 107, 117, 119

K

Kadesh-barnea 23
Khirbet Qeiyafa 53
Kidron Valley 17, 52, 73, 75, 77, 99, 103, 127, 131, 134
Kindling/Fuel Gate 77
Knights Templar 108, 114

L

Lake Huldah 23
Lampstand 8, 14, 30
Last Supper 45, 95
Laver (See also Molten Sea) 14, 29, 40, 77, 81, 82
Lebanon 24, 59
Levites 7, 26, 40, 51, 60, 81, 134

M

Maccabeus, Judas 63, 65, 110
Makheloth 23
Marah 23
Masada 98, 136
Mediterranean Sea 23
Megiddo 23
Memphis (Noph) 23
Menorah. *See* Lampstand
Mercy Seat 7, 9, 31, 41, 46, 87, 126
Messiah 5, 56, 65, 75, 80, 83, 93, 98, 100, 115, 123, 134, 136
Midian 23
Millennial Kingdom 65
Miphkad Gate 75
Miqva'ot. *See* Ritual Immersion Pools
Mishnah 16, 75, 80, 81, 82, 86

Moab 23
Molten Sea 29, 82
Monumental Staircase 69, 77, 100, 103, 127
Moors Gate 118, 121, 122, 127, 128
Moses 6, 7, 9, 20, 21, 31, 38, 40, 41, 44, 60, 115, 121, 132, 137
Most Holy Place. *See* Holy of Holies
Mt. Carmel 23
Mt. Gerizim 17, 61
Mt. Moriah 21, 31, 52, 59, 86, 87, 107, 126
Mt. Nebo 23
Mt. of Olives 75, 84, 95, 112, 113, 134
Mt. Sinai 9, 21, 23, 38
Mt. Zion. *See* Zion
Muhammad 1, 107, 109, 113, 115, 120, 121

N

Napoleon 115
Nazareth 23
Nebuchadnezzar 49, 51, 58, 65, 110
Negev 23
Nehemiah 22, 59, 60, 61, 65
New Jerusalem 5, 6, 132, 137, 138
Nicanor Gate 77, 81, 83
Night Journey of Muhammad 109, 113
Nile River 23
Noph (Memphis) 23
Northern Gate 77

O

Old City of Jerusalem 122
Olivet Discourse 95
Omar, Caliph 107, 110, 113
On 23
Onias II 63
Onias III 63
Orthodox Jews 1, 123
Ottoman Empire 108, 110, 114, 115, 116, 119, 122, 135

P

Palestine 115, 116, 128
Palestine Liberation Organization 116
Paphos 23
Passover 44, 45, 46, 51, 67, 73, 93, 94, 95, 99, 100
Paul, Apostle 5, 15, 42, 45, 46, 96, 137
Pen of Wood 81, 82
Pentecost 46, 78, 100

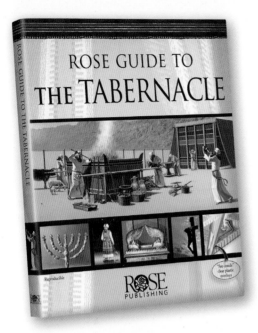

Rose Guide to the Tabernacle

Winner of the 2009 Christian Retailers' Choice Awards for Best Bible Reference and Study Book.

Full color, reproducible book on the The Tabernacle, with clear plastic overlays of the coverings of the "tent of meeting." The Tabernacle was the place where the Israelites worshiped God after the Exodus. Learn how the sacrifices, utensils, and even the structure of the tabernacle were designed to show us something about God. See the parallels between the Old Testament sacrifices and priests' duties, and Jesus' service as the perfect sacrifice and perfect high priest.

See how:
The Tabernacle was built
The sacrifices pointed towards Jesus Christ
The design of the tent revealed God's holiness and humanity's need for God
The Ark of the Covenant was at the center of worship.

Hardcover, 128 pages, full color, reproducible.   ISBN: 9781596362765

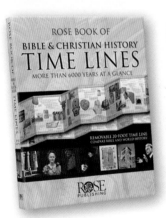 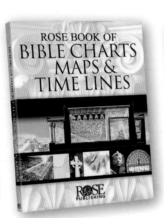 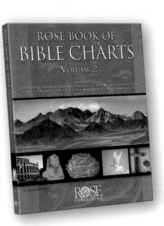 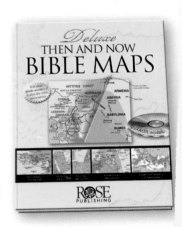

Rose Book of Bible & Christian History Time Lines
Rose Book of Bible Charts, Maps & Time Lines
Rose Book of Bible Charts Volume 2
Deluxe "Then and Now" Bible Maps

Hardcover.   ISBN: 9781596360846
Hardcover. 192 pages.   ISBN: 9781596360228
Hardcover. 233 pages.   ISBN: 9781596362758
Hardcover with CD-ROM.   ISBN: 9781596361638

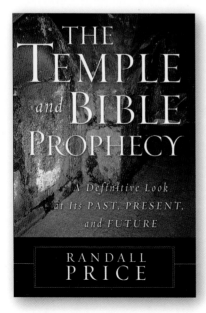

The Temple and Bible Prophecy:
A Definitive Look at its Past, Present, and Future
by Randall Price

This comprehensive study of the Jewish Temple helps readers answer these questions and more. It also provides: a fast-paced history of the Tabernacle, Solomon's Temple, Zerubbabel's Temple, and Herod's Temple an enlightening look at God's eternal purpose for the Temple a concise explanation of why the Temple disappeared and why it must reappear.

Available from World of the Bible Ministries, Inc. www.worldofthebible.com,
PO Box 827, San Marcos, TX 78667-0827. (512) 396-3799

Hardcover, 747 pages, 6 x 9 in, Harvest House Publishers, Inc.   ISBN: 0736913874

More from the author:
The Battle for the Last Days Temple, In Search of Temple Treasures,
The Coming Last Days Temple (DVD), In Search of Temple Treasures (DVD)